ADOPTION NOW

ADOPTION NOW

Messages from Research

JOHN WILEY & SONS, LTD
Chichester • New York • Weinheim • Brisbane • Singapore • Toronto

Other Wiley Editorial Offices
John Wiley & Sons, Inc., 605 Third Avenue,
New York, NY 10158-0012, USA

WILEY-VCH Verlag GmbH, Pappelallee 3,
D-69469 Weinheim, Germany

Jacaranda Wiley Ltd, 33 Park Road, Milton,
Queensland 4064, Australia

John Wiley & Sons (Asia) Pte Ltd, 2 Clementi Loop #02-01,
Jin Xing Distripark, Singapore 129809

John Wiley & Sons (Canada) Ltd, 22 Worcester Road,
Rexdale, Ontario M9W 1LI, Canada

ISBN 0-471-85204-X

Typeset in Optima and Melior by MHL Typesetting Ltd, Coventry
Project managed by Macfarlane Production Services, Markyate, Herts
Printed and bound in Great Britain by Alden Press, Oxford
This book is printed on acid-free paper responsibly manufactured from sustainable
forestry, in which at least two trees are planted for each one used for paper production.

Foreword

Good quality research is essential if the policy making process is to be effective. This is certainly the case with adoption. As the Government continues to develop policy in this area, it is important that we can draw upon the most up-to-date and reliable information. And this information needs to be widely shared with everyone with an interest in the welfare and well being of children.

This is precisely the purpose of *Adoption Now: Messages from Research*. The most recent and important studies on adoption have been brought together in a single volume, presented in a way that focuses on the main ingredients of each project. The particular subject areas are diverse; their outcomes are sometimes provocative and sometimes surprising but always informative and challenging. Its publication is timely. It coincides with the Quality Protects programme of which adoption is a key element. The Government believes very strongly in the positive role that adoption can play. As a Government, we are determined systematically to transform all services for children and to ensure that adoption becomes part of the mainstream of these services.

Adoption Now highlights many important aspects of adoption, not least the quality of services provided for children, delay in finding a suitable placement, recruitment of adoptive parents including single adopters, preparing children for adoption, placing siblings for adoption as well as the legal process. All those involved with children's services need to reflect upon these findings and ask themselves what it signifies for their own practice. The Government, for its part, will continue to pay the closest attention to improving adoption policy and practice. We owe the children concerned nothing less.

JOHN HUTTON
Parliamentary Under Secretary of State
Department of Health

This report has been prepared by Professor Roy Parker with the help of an advisory group. The group's membership included a broad range of those involved in providing homes through adoption, an adopted person and professionals. In addition, relevant drafts were read by the researchers whose work was reviewed, by other academics interested in the field and by policy makers, trainers and practitioners. The successful conclusion of the research programme was achieved as a result of the interest, enthusiasm and commitment of many people. In particular, the author would like to express his thanks to the Department of Health for its support and to Carolyn Davies, Michael Brennan, Julia Ridgway, Tom Jeffery and Heather Thorn for managing and organising the whole programme, and in particular to Pat Lees whose secretarial support has made the completion of this programme possible.

The advisory group

Chair:	Julia Ridgway, Social Services Inspector (Adoption Policy)
Department of Health:	Michael Brennan (Adoption Policy) Carolyn Davies (Research and Development Division)
Research:	Professor John Triseliotis, University of Glasgow Professor David Quinton, University of Bristol
Legal aspects:	Jennifer Jenkins (Member Adoption Law Review Group)
Directors of Social Services Departments	Andra Johnstone (Principal Officer) Newcastle Social Services Pennio Pennie, Lambeth Social Services Department
Voluntary Organisations:	Margaret Dight (Assistant Director) Catholic Children's Society, Nottingham
End User Groups:	Felicity Collier (Director) British Agencies for Adoption and Fostering
Managers and Practitioners:	Janet Denny (Principal Planning Officer) Birmingham Social Services Department Val Hales (Manager) Leeds Social Services Department
Users:	Nikki Kitcher (Adopted Person) Judy Jackson (Adopter)

Contents

Acknowledgements

Warm thanks are due to the members of the working party who were assiduous in combing through the reports and sharing their views. Yet the reports could not have been produced without the generous collaboration of many children, adopters, practitioners and organisations. The researchers themselves gave the working party considerable assistance in their comments on drafts and in providing the brief summaries of their studies – always a difficult task.

Particular thanks go to Patricia Lees for her work in keeping the minutes of the working party's deliberations and to her and to Yvonne McCann for their tireless efforts in preparing the material for publication. Thanks are also due to Heather Thorn of the Department of Health for her support in facilitating the arrangements for the working party. Professor Parker would also like to record his gratitude to members of the Research Unit and the Centre for Social Policy at Dartington for their support and assistance.

Preface

This overview of the main messages to emerge from the research on adoption that has been funded by the Research and Development division of the Department of Health over the last decade and commissioned and managed by Carolyn Davies who initiated this overview. It is the sixth of such summaries. Previous reports have dealt with other aspects of child care.[1] The purpose of these publications is to ensure that the results of the various studies on the subject are brought together in a way that shows what is likely to be relevant to the work of practitioners, managers and those responsible for policy.

In this case the Department established a working party, chaired by Julia Ridgway of the Social Services Inspectorate, and composed largely of those directly engaged in adoption. Each study was read by at least three members of the group, who then reported back what they considered to be the most important findings for practice and policy. In doing so they also indicated how much confidence they felt could be placed in particular results and the extent to which these accorded with their own experience. A record was kept of the discussions that followed. It was with the help and guidance of these reports and deliberations that Professor Roy Parker wrote the final document.

Like its predecessors in the series, *Adoption Now* is not a review of the adoption literature or even a review of all the relevant research. These can be found elsewhere.[2] However, where it seemed particularly appropriate, reference is made to studies other than those which were part of the Department of Health's programme.

---

1 The previous reports were: *Social Work Decisions in Child Care* (1985), HMSO; *Patterns and Outcomes in Child Placement* (1991), HMSO; *Child Protection: Messages from Research* (1995), HMSO; *Focus on Teenagers* (1996), HMSO; and *Caring for Children Away from Home* (1998), Wiley.

2 For example, Triseliotis J, Shireman J and Hundleby M (1997), *Adoption: Theory, Policy and Practice*, Cassell; Sellick C and Thoburn J (1997), *What Works in Family Placement?* Barnardos; and Thoburn J (1992), Review of Research Relating to Adoption, Appendix C, *Review of Adoption Law: Report to Ministers of an Inter-departmental Working Party*, Department of Health. Also, most of the studies contain reviews of the literature and research relevant to their concerns.

This report is, therefore, a distillation of what the working party regarded as the most important and reliable findings of this *particular* set of studies. Appendix 1 contains the summaries of the projects which were prepared in collaboration with each of the teams. We hope that both these and the report which follows will encourage people to read the studies in full. No summaries, however carefully made, can do justice to the rich detail which they contain.

1

Introduction

Setting the context

The last 25 years have seen a dramatic change in the character of adoption. Its most significant feature has been the sharp reduction, from the 1970s onwards, in the number of babies of unmarried mothers being given up for adoption. There were several reasons for this.[1]

First, there was the 'contraception revolution', accelerated by the increasing use of the 'pill' from the early 1960s. Then, in 1967, the Abortion Act extended the grounds upon which a legal abortion could be obtained. The number of such abortions doubled in England and Wales in the first five years after the implementation of the Act and reached a peak of 175,000 a year in the early 1990s. In 1995 a fifth of all conceptions were terminated, and a third of those amongst unmarried women.[2]

Gradually, the stigma associated with illegitimacy diminished, a trend reflected in the Family Law Reform Act 1987. It had been this sense of stigma which had persuaded many unmarried mothers to give up their babies for adoption. Indeed, during the 1950s and 1960s around a fifth of all children who were born illegitimate were adopted by strangers, mostly as babies.[3]

In addition to these changes the status of unmarried motherhood came to be absorbed into the rapidly growing number of 'lone mothers' which followed the relaxation of the grounds for divorce introduced in the Divorce Law Reform Act 1969. The new terminology of 'one-parent families'[4] marked the increasing incorporation of unmarried motherhood into this all-embracing category. The issues of illegitimacy and its attendant stigma were fast disappearing, subsumed into the new concern about lone parenthood, a concern partly aroused by the poverty with which it was often accompanied.

---

1 This analysis is informed by Kiernan K, Land H and Lewis J (1998), *Lone Motherhood in Twentieth-Century Britain*, Oxford.

2 ONS (1998), *Social Trends 28*, Stationery Office; table 2.27.

3 Leete R (1978), Adoption Trends and Illegitimate Births, 1951–77, *Population Trends* 14, OPCS, HMSO.

4 See Finer (1974) *Report of the Committee on One-Parent Families*, vol 1, Cmnd 5629.

Another factor which contributed to the reduction in the number of babies of unmarried mothers who were given up for adoption was the shift in attitudes to sexual morality and to the institution of marriage. This was manifested in a considerable increase in the number of births outside marriage. Indeed, by the middle of the 1990s they accounted for a third of all births. Such births became commonplace and, given their scale, unmarried motherhood could no longer be regarded as 'a special problem of the deviant few' attributable to moral laxity or psychological disturbance and emotional immaturity, diagnoses which had helped to sustain its stigmatised status. Unmarried mothers were no longer exposed to the social pressures that had obliged many of them to agree to the adoption of their babies.

There were, finally, various changes in housing and social security policies, especially in the 1970s, that eased (although they by no means eliminated) some of the practical problems of bringing up a child single-handedly. Steps were taken to give lone parents better access to council housing, and their position within the income maintenance system was improved by changes introduced in the Child Benefit Act 1975.

Thus, as a result of these converging trends, the character of unmarried motherhood underwent a radical transformation, starting in the 1960s. Over much the same period, however, changes were also occurring in the way in which the well-being of vulnerable children was being perceived.

First, there was a growing conviction, which has continued to be supported by experience and research, that children should not be separated from their parents and family if at all possible. This encouraged efforts to restore to their families children who had been separated from them, a principle codified in the Children Act 1948 but only gradually put into practice. This was followed somewhat later by the official encouragement of preventive work which was aimed at avoiding the need for such separation in the first place, a development that was given legal endorsement in the Children Act 1963 but which, again, took time to gather momentum.

To the extent that these two policies – of restoration and prevention – were successful, the circumstances of the children coming into and remaining in local authority care became more problematic than those of the children who had preceded them. Of course, neither policy was pursued with equal vigour in all areas; but their cumulative effect, certainly after 1978 with the downturn in the number of children in care, was to increase the proportion who were considered to have 'special needs'. These children tended to be older and to have had more chequered and damaging childhoods. Furthermore, the emphasis upon rehabilitation also meant that social workers were expected to persevere in their efforts to secure the safe return of children to their families, thereby delaying the point at which any other plan was made for their future if that became necessary.

However, the 1970s saw a growing concern that steps should be taken to ensure that children like these had a stable home, reliable relationships and committed and enduring care. In 1973 Rowe and Lambert published *Children Who Wait*[5] which showed that many children were indeed languishing in care for want of effective planning. Some, it was argued, could have rejoined their families; others required a long-term alternative. At much the same time the notion of 'permanency planning' was arriving in Britain from the United States. This, in particular, was thought to advocate adoption as the best permanent solution for separated children who could not, within a reasonable time, be rehabilitated with their families.

These ideas found expression in the Children Act 1975 and then in the Adoption Act 1976. In essence this made it easier for children who were in the care of local authorities to be adopted where that was appropriate. It also required each local authority to ensure that an adoption service was provided in their area. However, the legislation was not implemented until 1988, although by then most authorities had such a service as it was then understood to be.[6]

Nevertheless, there was no substantial increase in the *number* of adoptions from care until after 1988. A peak of 2700 was reached in 1992, falling back thereafter to 1900 in 1996, although rising again slightly to 2000 in 1998.[7] This fall, it has been claimed, was attributable to the effect of the Children Act 1989 which was implemented in October, 1991. It was reported that local authorities then became more hesitant to recommend adoption, believing that the courts would now only be prepared to grant an order if there was indisputable evidence that a child's rehabilitation with their family was impossible or unwise.

However, adoptions from care came to account for an increasingly large *proportion* of all adoptions: from just 7% in 1975 to around 40% during the 1990s with most of the others being adoptions by step-parents or relatives. The current picture is set out diagrammatically in the figure opposite.

Although there were fewer babies being relinquished for adoption, by the second half of the 1970s social services departments were being encouraged to consider adoption for more of the children in their care, more of whom were

---

5 Rowe J and Lambert L (1973), *Children Who Wait*, Association of British Adoption Agencies.

6 See DHSS, Circular LAC (87) 8, *Adoption Act 1976: Implementation.*

7 Department of Health, *Children Looked After by Local Authorities – England.*

The pattern of adoption in England and Wales, 1996–7

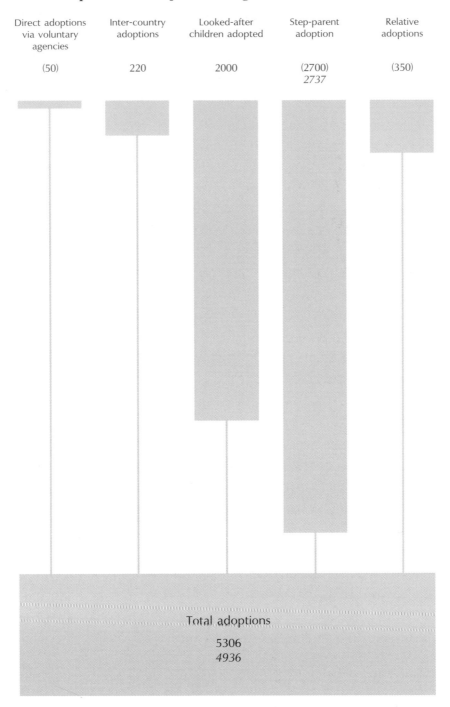

Note: The figures in brackets are estimates. Those in italics are from the Judicial Statistics where these differ from, or are additional to, those published by the ONS.

Sources: (a) Office for National Statistics (1999), *Marriage, Divorce and Adoption Statistics*, FM2.24, Stationery Office. (b) Lord Chancellor's Dept (1997), *Judicial Statistics*, Cm 3716, Stationery Office. (c) Department of Health (1998), *Children Looked After in England*, and Welsh Office (1997).

older and regarded as having special needs. The characteristics of the children who could be considered for adoption therefore had changed in a far-reaching fashion. Rather than children being 'available' for adoption, the emphasis shifted to finding families for those children who needed a permanent home. Adoption came to be acknowledged in official and professional circles primarily as a means of meeting the needs of certain children rather than as a solution to the problem of unmarried motherhood or to the needs of infertile couples.

For all these reasons it is plain that the institution of adoption has undergone profound changes, changes that have brought with them new challenges. Many more adoptions are now contested; the selection of adopters and their suitability for particular children with particular needs demands more exacting assessment; once adopted, more children continue to have some form of contact with their birth families; and the need for adoptive parents and their children to be offered support after the order has been granted places special demands upon social and other services. In the past it has been assumed that having adopted a baby or infant with the agreement of the birth parents, and with all contact having been discontinued and secrecy preserved, the adopters could be left to raise the child as they would a child born to them; that is, without any special services needing to be provided. Such an assumption is no longer tenable.

It was the emergence of issues like these, and the failure of the law to reflect them, which prompted the Adoption Law Review that was set in train in 1989.[8] Three of the studies reviewed here were commissioned by the Department of Health with the intention that they should contribute to this reconsideration. Others, commissioned somewhat later, continued to reflect the need to understand better the nature and implications of the changing character of adoption, changes that were acknowledged in the proposals for reform set out in the 1993 white paper *Adoption: the Future*[9] and in the subsequent draft bill published in 1996 but taken no further. Since then a circular,[10] several reports prepared by the Social Services Inspectorate[11] and the latest government

---

8 See Department of Health (1992), *Review of Adoption Law: Report to Ministers of an Inter-departmental Working Group*.

9 Department of Health, Welsh Office, Home Office, Lord Chancellor's Department (1993), *Adoption: the Future*, Cm 2288.

10 Department of Health, *Adoption: Achieving the Right Balance*, circular LAC (98) 20.

11 For example, Department of Health, Social Services Inspectorate (1996), *For Children's Sake: an SSI Inspection of Local Authority Adoption Services*, and part 2 (1997), *An Inspection of Local Authority Post-Placement and Post Adoption Services*. Also (1995), *Moving Goalposts: A Study of Post-Adoption Contact in the North of England*.

initiative entitled *Quality Protects* have highlighted the need for adoption to be treated as an integral part of the child care system and for attention to be paid to the repercussions of its changing character. It is this new climate that makes it particularly important for the messages from the Department of Health's programme of adoption research to be widely spread.

The character of the studies

All the studies considered in the Department of Health's programme took as their starting point placements which had been made or where the adoption process had begun. In doing so they were able to address many of the key issues which surround adoption today; for example, shortcomings (such as delay) in the adoption procedures; the adequacy and impact of the way in which children and adopters are prepared; the matching of the child's needs with the adopters' resources (including the placement of children from minority ethnic backgrounds); the nature of the problems with which children and adopters are beset; the kinds of support that adoption now entails, and the factors which are associated with more or less successful placements (including the placement of siblings). The key features of the studies are set out in the table opposite.

Although the studies varied in their design and sample sizes, as well as when they were conducted, there were many findings which converged and other results that had the virtue of plausibility, which suggested lines of development and reconsideration, or which confirmed the conclusions of earlier studies. One of the particular strengths of the programme was that three of the studies gathered the views of some 80 children, and all but one of the projects collected information directly from adopters, either through postal questionnaires or personal interviews. Some also elicited the views of social workers, agency managers and solicitors. However, none of the studies obtained the views of the birth relatives, although information about them is to be found in most of the reports.

Despite the many issues that the studies addressed there were some important matters which they did not. These were questions pertaining to the period before adoption proceedings began, questions such as: for which of the children for whom local authorities carry responsibility is adoption appropriate? When should that decision be taken? Is adoption better than the alternative options and how, in any case, can that be established? What factors convince a local authority that a child in their care should be adopted? What

The studies considered and their main features

	Size of main sample	Date of placements/applications	Age of children	Period of follow-up	Control/comparison group	Adoption and fostering?
Lowe N, Murch M et al. Supporting Adoption. Referred to as the Lowe and Murch study and occasionally as the Support study	Agency study 1557 Family study 226	1992–4	Agency study all ages Family study 5-plus	1 year after order	No	No
Lowe N et al. Freeing for Adoption. Referred to as the Freeing study	150	1985–7	All ages	n/a	No	No
Malos E and Milsom L, Delays and Difficulties in the Judicial Process in Adoption. Referred to as the Malos and Milsom study	192	1992–4	All ages	n/a	No	No
Murch M, Lowe N et al. Pathways to Adoption. Referred to as the Pathways study	1268	1986–8	All ages	n/a	No	No
Owen M, Adoption by Single People. Referred to as the Owen study	48	Various	All ages	Various	Yes	No
Quinton D, Rushton A et al. Adoption and Fostering in Middle Childhood. Referred to as the Quinton and Rushton study	61	Early 90s	5–9	1 year after placement	Yes	Yes
Rutter M et al. The English and Romanian Adoption Study. Referred to as the Romanian study	165	Early 90s	up to 42 months	at 4 and at 6	Yes	No
Rushton A, Dance C et al. Children's Relationships in Late Permanent Placements (siblings). Referred to as the Rushton and Dance study	133 (72 groups)	1994–5	5–11	1 year after placement	Yes	Yes
Thoburn J et al. Permanent Family Placement for Children of Minority Ethnic Origin. Referred to as the Thoburn study	297	1979–86	All ages	10 years after placement	No	Yes
Thomas C, Beckford V et al, Adopted Children Speaking. Referred to as the Thomas and Beckford study	41	Various	5 and over	Various	No	No

deters them from taking this step and, in any case, which looked-after children will never be candidates?

Similarly, none of the studies looked specifically at how certain people had reached the point of having a child placed with them for adoption. Who do not persist in their enquiries or application, and why? Who, with advice, do not pursue an application and who are not approved? These are important questions, the answers to which are needed in order to inform recruitment campaigns or to gain an accurate view of the extent to which social workers actually have the kind of choice of adopters that appropriate 'matching' implies.

Some cautionary notes

It is necessary at the outset to appreciate the differences in the aims and design of the various studies, and for these to be borne in mind throughout when conclusions are being drawn. There are seven points in particular to be made.

Adoption and foster placements were not always clearly distinguished   Three of the studies (Quinton and Rushton, Thoburn, and Rushton and Dance) had mixed samples of adoptive and foster placements. As will be seen, there were certain differences between these two groups.

Some of the studies omitted placements that had broken down   Thoburn and her colleagues excluded all the placements that had disrupted in their first two years from her 'interview' sample and, having based their studies on current placements, neither Owen nor Thomas and Beckford could include past disruptions. Furthermore, most of the researchers acknowledged that it was likely that the placements about which they were unable to obtain information included a number which had broken down and that they were likely, therefore, to have been under-represented in the results.

The studies covered children of different ages   Given the known significance of age at placement to outcomes, it is important to keep in mind how this differed from study to study. Indeed, most of them were concerned with children of school age although, in 1998, nearly half of the looked-after children who were adopted were under five, albeit few were less than a year.[12] Likewise, most of the children adopted from overseas will be under five.

Some categories of children were excluded   Neither the Quinton and Rushton nor the Thomas and Beckford studies included children with severe (undefined) physical disabilities. The former also left out those with severe learning difficulties. Rushton and Dance omitted sibling placements in which at least one of the children had a profound mental or physical disability.

The studies covered different times and therefore reflected different policies and practices   Not all the studies were based upon what was happening in the 1990s. Two drew upon samples taken from the 1980s. Thoburn's follow-up

12 *Children Looked After by Local Authorities, 1998.*

study was based upon a sample of placements originally made between 1980 and 1984, whilst the *Pathways* research obtained its sample from adoption and freeing applications made in the years 1986 to 1988. Both Owen and Thomas and Beckford, looking as they were at current placements, included children who had been in their families for varying periods between one and 11 years.

The assessments of outcomes were made at different times   The periods over which the placements were assessed were not the same. This is important since different durations may well lead to more or less optimistic conclusions. Both the Quinton and Rushton and the Rushton and Dance studies reported outcomes at 12 months after placement. Those based on the Romanian children did so when the children were aged four and then again at six. Thoburn made her assessments 10 years after the original placements. The Lowe and Murch study followed up the placements for one year after the order was made.

The assessments of outcomes were made in different ways   Apart from Owen and Thomas and Beckford, all the researchers reported on the level of conventionally defined disruptions. Over and above this, however, most endeavoured to construct or to apply a variety of more sophisticated measures which emphasised different aspects of the placements' progress.

The report

The chapters which follow are arranged broadly to reflect the topics dealt with by most of the studies. However, the headings, such as 'preparation' or 'support', should not be taken to imply quite separate features of the adoption process. In the first place they can be interpreted differently by different people and, in the second, they are not as exclusive as the divisions suggest; there is a good deal of overlap, both in the issues and in the chronology. Nevertheless, this arrangement was chosen as probably the most convenient for the reader.

Where appropriate, each chapter begins with an illustrative summary of what the children had to say. Many of their observations were both moving and instructive but, above all, they warned against sweeping generalisations, drew attention to some of the matters which adults are liable to overlook or to discount, and emphasised how important it is that we listen to what they have to say.

2

Outcomes, predictors and risks

Outcomes

Disruption

Most of the studies reported the rate of 'disruption'[1] amongst the placements in their samples. However, disruptions are not necessarily the most sensitive indicators of outcomes. In the first place there is the question of definition. If a 16 year-old decides to move out after living most of his life in his adoptive home is that a disruption or not? Secondly, the quality of the experience whilst the placement lasts obviously affects how an eventual disruption should be evaluated. Thirdly, there is the issue of whether or not a disruption implies a severance of relationships. A child may leave but continue to have a supportive and enduring connection with the adoptive family. The simple 'rate of disruption' cannot reflect these variations, although from the interviews, especially those in the Thoburn study, it is plain that they exist. For example, she observed that

> some of the placements which appeared ... to have broken down could be seen, in the light of the information we received about earlier severe problems and later progress and improvement in life chances, to have been successful. On the other hand, some of the placements which did not actually break down before the young people reached the age of 18 did not provide them with a 'family for life'.

The rates of disruption in the studies ranged from 2% to 24%; but it would be dangerous to regard them as comparable. The main sample sizes varied between 52 and 1557; and children's ages varied too. The placements were made at various times throughout the 1980s and 1990s when different policies and practices prevailed. More of the recent studies included adoptions by

---

1 The term 'disruption' is widely used but not always to describe the same thing. Usually it implies a breakdown that leads to the child leaving; but there can, of course, be a good deal of disruption (or disruptive behaviour) where the child remains with the family.

children's foster carers, amongst which disruption rates are likely to be low. Finally, any disruption rate must be related to the length of time that the children have been in their placements. The longer they have continued, the higher the eventual overall rate of breakdown is liable to be, especially as children reach adolescence. However, there is evidence from the Lowe and Murch study that rates may also be high in the time *before* an adoption order is made. Nine per cent of the 1557 placements recorded in their agency sample (covering children of all ages) had broken down,[2] but 92% of these had done so before the order. Three per cent more occurred in the first year after that and 5% thereafter. It is also notable that Thoburn and her colleagues discovered that only 77% of those in her large cohort who had been placed for adoption had actually gone on to be adopted by the family, although some had remained as foster children. These are important findings which, if they reflect what happens generally, have important implications for practice, not least in emphasising the need for careful selection and for dealing with the considerable stresses associated with the period of transition.

Unfortunately, only the Lowe and Murch study distinguished between disruptions that occurred before and after the adoption order had been granted, although Quinton and Rushton found that the new parents who had not made an application for an adoption order by the end of a year were those most likely to be facing difficulties.

The case studies of disruptions provided in several of the studies showed that the precipitating problems were severe. Indeed, Lowe and Murch concluded that the children whose placements had broken down had needed help before being placed for adoption, adding that 'risking yet another disruption in their lives in the light of their case histories appears desperate since it can only have added to the enormous problems [they] ... already had.' The fact that, over the short term, disruption rates were comparatively low should not obscure what they meant for those involved. Nor should all the provisos about the interpretation of such rates be forgotten.

The assessment of outcomes other than by reference to disruption

Several of the studies endeavoured to assess the outcomes of the placements in ways which did not rely on whether or not they survived. Although the

---

2 It is pointed out that agencies do not always know when a placement disrupts, particularly if it does so after the adoption order. By contrast, all those which occur before then will be known.

approaches differed they fell into five broad groups, often combined in a single project. First, there were those which measured the progress that children had made over the period of the follow-up. For example, Quinton and Rushton found that 36% of the children (5–9 years of age) had shown a reduction in adverse symptoms over a year; for 31% there had been little change, and for 33% their problems had worsened. Had an overall figure been reported however, the conclusion would have been 'no change', the number who had made progress being cancelled out by the number whose problems had increased.

The Romanian study also measured the progress of a group of children who 'were more severely deprived, physically and psychologically, than almost any other sizeable group of children previously studied'. However, at four years of age the physical 'catch-up' of those who had come to the UK under two was 'very substantial' and their developmental (cognitive) recovery was equally impressive, although it was 'not quite complete' in those who arrived after six months of age. However, although physical and cognitive progress had been outstanding there was some increase in problems of attention, motivation and behaviour. When assessed again at six years of age the various improvements were found to have been maintained, but few further gains were discernible.

Another group of Romanian children who had joined their new families between 24 and 42 months of age was assessed for the first time when they were six years old and although their physical and cognitive recovery was also considerable it was less than that of those who had arrived when they were younger. For example, a much larger proportion of the older arrivals had been 'statemented' or had received special educational or health services by the time they were six. In both groups, however, there was evidence of problems with peer relations and some atypical and aberrant behaviour towards adults.

The second approach to determining outcomes was for the researchers to assess the stability or security of the placements at certain points. In the Quinton and Rushton study, for example, 72% of the placements were considered to have been stable at the end of 12 months, although not without their difficulties. In the Rushton and Dance enquiry into sibling placements (where children were between five and 11) 80% of the children appeared to have had a stable position in the family at the end of a year. Alongside this measure of outcomes the new parents were also asked to assess the degree of mutual attachment that had been achieved after a year. For 43% this was said to be good; for 30% it appeared to be developing, but for 27% it was considered to be poor.

A third approach, which was adopted in the Romanian study for example, was to ask parents how satisfied they were with the child as a member of the family. There was a high level of satisfaction amongst the adopters of the children entering the UK under 24 months: 91% were markedly positive. In the control group of domestic adoptions of children placed under six months satisfaction was almost total.

Since some of the studies conducted detailed interviews with the parents and with the children they provided an opportunity for the researchers to assess the 'success' of the placement from their observations. This represented a fourth approach to assessing outcomes. For example, eight of the 51 placements in her interview group were rated by Thoburn as having been highly successful; 16 as successful; 13 as successful in most respects; 10 in some respects and four as unsuccessful. In applying a more rigorous assessment based upon 11 dimensions of 'well-being', five of the children were rated as being above average and 26 as average. The well-being of 16 was judged to have been below average and for four poor. The results differed, however, depending upon *which* aspect of well-being was being considered. For example, 36 of the children were in good health; 31 had a clear sense of their ethnic identity and 23 had no emotional or behavioural problems.

Such variations on the different dimensions of 'well-being' are a valuable reminder that overall assessments of outcomes may be misleading, even for the individual child: the placements may have been successful with regard, say, to education but not as far as attachments are concerned. It is often assumed that progress on one front augers well for progress on another, and for certain combinations this is supported by research; but it may not hold true for *all* combinations. Nor is it apparent that all dimensions of a child's well-being should necessarily be accorded the same weight.

Some of the studies built in control groups of one kind or another or used existing survey data in order to compare the adopted children's well-being with that of other children, and this represented a fifth approach to assessing outcomes. For example, the results that Owen obtained from applying the 'Looking After Children' schedules to her sample were compared with those derived from the 'community group' that was used to test the LAC materials.[3] This was a sample of families and children that excluded any who were, or had been, in contact with a social services department. On the basis of such comparisons the results were encouraging. For example, 87% of the adopted children were said to get on very well with their parent; in the community group the proportion had been 77%. Eighty-four per cent were shown physical affection in contrast to 63% of the comparison children. Black, white and

---

3 See, Ward H (ed) (1995), *Looking After Children: Research into Practice*, HMSO.

mixed-race children scored equally highly with respect to their sense of identity, and no differently from the community group. In the light of the fact that 21% of the children were physically or mentally disabled and that half had learning difficulties, the 'outcomes' on the health and educational fronts were considered to be 'remarkable'.

The Romanian study team compared the children in their sample with a control group of UK baby adoptions at four and at six, and although they had made considerable progress they remained significantly 'behind' this parallel group on all the dimensions of outcome. Likewise, both they and the Quinton and Rushton team compared the behaviour at school of the children in their samples with that of classmates and found considerably more problems.

The variety of these different approaches to assessing outcome reflect the complexity of the concept. None of the studies provides a categorical answer to the question 'how well do adoptions succeed?' However, the assessments which were more sophisticated than those based simply on disruptions did demonstrate the complicated way in which the successful aspects of placements could be found alongside other more worrying features. Although the periods over which most of the researchers made their assessments were quite short, the more sensitive indicators of outcome also provided evidence for both improvement *and* deterioration over time.

The Main Points

The difference between the samples in the studies makes the reliable estimation of *overall* rates of disruption impossible.

Disruption is only one indicator of outcome. Other measures which assess more subtle aspects of placements provide a more useful basis for policy and practice, especially the deployment of supportive services. Even so, generalisations derived from rather different studies should be treated with caution.

Predictors

All those concerned with the engineering of successful adoptions are anxious to have a reliable means of knowing 'what works': which factors best distinguish the better from the less good outcomes. Of course, as Quinton and Rushton point out, 'we are very far from possessing the kind of knowledge that could be used as a rule of thumb for practitioners'. Nevertheless, their study and others do take us further forward, despite the considerable difficulty in unravelling the effect of so many different influences. Indeed, one message that stands out above all others is that there is no single factor which leads to success or to instability in a placement, but rather the way in which several factors combine and interact.

There was a good deal of similarity between all these studies in the predictive factors which they identified, although some were more prominent in one project than another. However, there was no instance where the results were contradictory. Some of the studies undertook multi-variate analyses which enabled the overlap between variables to be identified whilst others did not. Hence, some were better able to reduce the number of 'key' predictors.

The child's age at placement   The younger the child the less likelihood was there of a poor outcome. For example, in the Thoburn research over a follow-up period of 10 years the disruption rate was 10% for those who were placed under four but 40% for those who were nine or over. Even in the Romanian study those entering the UK under 24 months of age had generally made more progress than those who were older on arrival (up to 42 months). Furthermore, it should be noted that up to the age of six there were no disruptions amongst the younger group or amongst the control group of domestic adoptions of children under six months. Since most of the other studies restricted themselves to older children within quite narrow bands, age was less likely to emerge as a discriminator of outcome.

The child's past experience   The longer children had been looked after in care and the greater the number of their moves were both considered to be indicators of high risk in the Lowe and Murch study. However, although a history of multiple moves was significantly associated with disruption in the Thoburn study it was subsumed into the set of other factors after multi-variate analysis.

There were, however, other features of the child's past experience that emerged as important predictors. In the Quinton and Rushton work the child's earlier rejection by the birth parents (often when new partnerships were formed and when other siblings or half siblings remained at home), increased the risk of instability in the placement considerably. The Rushton and Dance team reached the same conclusion. Of course, rejection may be hard to identify consistently, but the fact of brothers and sisters still being at home should alert social workers to its possibility.

Several studies include abuse or severe deprivation amongst the factors with a predictive value; the Thoburn research for example, but especially the

Romanian project. The latter noted that less progress had been made by those children who had been exposed to the longest periods of deprivation, its severity having been rather similar for all of them.

The children's behaviour   Behaviour problems of various kinds were associated with poorer outcomes but, in the Quinton and Rushton, Rushton and Dance and the Romanian studies, the child's hyperactivity, restlessness and inability to concentrate emerged as particularly important. Defiant, aggressive or sexualised behaviours were also indicators of risk in several of the studies. One of the 'high risk' factors in the Lowe and Murch study, for example, was the child's violent or sexually abusive behaviour towards other children.

The composition of the adoptive family household   Since many of the children were placed in already established families there were other children to be taken into account. Virtually all the studies found that the presence of birth children increased the risk of poorer outcomes. Some, however, reported that the age differences mattered whilst others did not. The Romanian study also found that at four the families with closely spaced *biological* children were expressing increased 'negative evaluation', but that by the time the adopted child was six this had reduced, suggesting some adaptation over time or different developmental stages. Likewise, in some cases in the other studies the risk associated with there being birth children in the family diminished as time passed. However, the presence in the household of other unrelated adopted children was not a negative indicator, nor was the fact that a child was placed with his or her birth siblings. Indeed, several studies suggested that this was a 'protective' factor. Conversely, the splitting up of siblings who had been part of a settled sibling group emerged as a risk factor in the Lowe and Murch study.

Parenting styles   Quinton and Rushton found the style of parenting to be significantly associated with different outcomes. In particular, the level of parents' 'responsiveness' made a difference, the key elements of that responsiveness being their expressed warmth, their emotional involvement and sensitivity, and the way in which these were combined.

However, none of these predictive factors stood alone; there was a considerable degree of interaction. For example, the parents in established families tended to be less responsive than those in child-free families and this was not necessarily accounted for by the kinds of children they received; rejected children did better with responsive parenting; the style of parenting was likely to be affected by the child's behaviour, especially by the degree of attachment that had been formed; if children were separated from their siblings at placement they did better in child-free families; for those placed alone, the experience of having been rejected was related to instability in the placement, and it was more difficult for those children to settle who had been abused and placed together.

Of course, predictions are not certainties; simply checking through such factors will not be enough to ensure a successful placement; but if not sufficient it is certainly necessary.

The Main Points

A detailed and accurate history of a child's background must be obtained, especially whether or not he or she has experienced rejection by the birth family, has sexually abused other children, or is over-active. It is also important to know the duration and nature of the deprivations that have been suffered as well as the pattern of previous disruptions and other broken attachments.

The composition of the prospective adoptive household must be taken into account, especially the ages, status and attitudes of any birth children.

Experience based upon bringing up their birth children may not be a sufficiently reliable guide to parents' ability successfully to adopt a child posing the kinds of challenges that are now common.

The parenting style of the prospective adopters must be explored; in particular, the likely level of their 'responsiveness', a matter that may well be affected by the need to retain a balance in their affections between their birth children and their adopted children. However, social workers need guidance on how parenting styles may be assessed.

Much turns on the way in which the elements of a child's background affect their behaviour and how this interacts with the parenting style of the adopters and the composition of their households.

None of these predictive indicators *alone* should shape placement decisions. Their implications should always be considered in conjunction with each other.

Risks

Given the disrupted backgrounds and the older ages of most of the children in these studies, the issue of the risks that may accompany their placements must be confronted. However, that issue has several dimensions.

When we endeavour to estimate risks what do we have in mind? The risk of disruption; the risk that a child's needs will not be met or the risk of problems being exacerbated? Furthermore, who is it who runs the risks? Obviously, the principal concern is with the child; but there is evidence that others in the adoptive family may also be exposed to a variety of risks. The parents may risk long periods of stress, frustration or despair. Other children in the family may be put at risk of unhappiness or, in some cases, abuse. They may feel that they risk the loss of their parents' attention or affection. The family as a whole may risk turbulence, upheaval and discord.

However, the negative aspects of risk can be counterbalanced by positive factors. No suggested placement will have a wholly negative or wholly positive set of possibilities, and these need to be considered alongside each other. Which advantages are likely to offset which disadvantages, and vice versa?

The estimation of the level of risk associated with a placement is a complicated professional task to be undertaken using the best available evidence; but that is not the end of the matter. What, for any particular child, is an *acceptable* level of risk? What is the cut-off point? Answers will depend on judgements that have regard to the risks associated with the main alternative courses of action and which take account of the likelihood that risks can be reduced by skilled support or whether, should they become a reality, there is a plan for dealing with the consequences. 'Acceptable' levels of risk will also be influenced by prevailing assumptions and expectations in local and national policies and by the resources available to offer more appropriate alternatives.

The Main Points

The nature and level of any risks associated with a proposed placement should be acknowledged. As well as the professionals, potential adopters need to be able to decide what risks they are willing to take, on their own behalf and that of their families.

There is a difference between alerting prospective adopters to the general kinds of risks accompanying adoption and those that relate specifically to the placement of a *particular* child in their *particular* family. Conveying the first caution without amending it in the light of an actual proposition can be misleading.

The satisfactions accompanying adoption for both children and adults should not be underestimated. They may serve to offset the risks.

The identification of possible risks can assist in planning the kind of support that may be needed once a placement is made.

3

Preparation

What the children had to say

Many children who had been adopted several years beyond babyhood recalled being anxious and frightened by the prospect unless, and until, they had met those who were to become their new parents. In this respect the children who were being adopted by their foster carers had a clear advantage. Those who were not, frequently recollected having been worried about what lay in store and especially about the changes they would have to face. Some wanted to stay with their foster carers. As one girl (9) in the Thomas and Beckford study explained, for example, 'I didn't want to move. I wanted to stay with [my foster parents], 'cause I'd been moved around so much'. Reassurances from social workers or foster carers that all would be well helped, but were not enough to dispel anxiety. Although the children did not always recall how adoption had been explained to them at the outset, it was plain that for many the concept had been difficult to grasp. One little girl thought it was a bit like getting married.

Nonetheless, the children had wanted to know about the family and place to which they were going. What were the adopters like? If there were other children, what were they like? What was the house like and the locality? What kind of school would they be attending? Of course, until a specific family had been chosen, adoption could remain no more than an idea, with all its uncertainties. Once there was a family about which children could be given information, some of these uncertainties could be removed; but that depended upon what was provided and upon how it was conveyed. Photographs and videos helped a lot, as did 'books' about themselves that adopters had compiled.

As well as wanting to have as much information about their future families as possible the children also recalled wanting the adopters to know about them: what their likes and dislikes were; something about their past (but not necessarily everything); and what upset or frightened them. Some had wanted to say what they hoped for with respect to contact with their birth families or their racial and cultural community. A few had prepared folders or videos telling the adopters about themselves.

First meetings with prospective adopters had often been approached with great trepidation. Will they like me? Will I like them? What should I say? How long will it take? Many felt shy and awkward, and some recognised that the adopters were likely to have felt the same. Others made the point that they found it difficult meeting new people anyway, especially in strange surroundings.

Visits and contacts thereafter were usually remembered as being rather easier; but some of the children said that they had continued to be anxious about making a good impression and because they were not clear what purpose the visits were supposed to serve. Were they to provide an opportunity for them to say whether they wanted to go to this family or not? Or were they to let the adopters decide whether they wanted them? Were they on trial? Some received contradictory messages.

Waiting for the final move was also remembered as an anxious time. The longer it had gone on the more anxious some had become. Would the adoption actually happen? Why was it delayed? A few children said that everything had been too hurried. Even those who had been looking forward to adoption could feel sadness at parting from foster carers. Others were upset at having to leave brothers and sisters, school friends and other children in the foster or residential home. Children, it should not have to be said, have attachments, social networks, familiar places and 'things' which they will be loth to leave, especially in the face of a largely unknown alternative.

Even after settling in the children's anxieties were not over. There was the waiting period before going to court for the final hearing, during which time there could be considerable apprehension and sometimes fear about what that involved as well as what the outcome would be. Some of that apprehension may well have been passed on by their adopters, particularly where there had been earlier contested hearings. Furthermore, in the minds of many of the children there was a clear association between courts and wrongdoing. The images that children had had were mainly those of criminal courts. They could be anxious about the judge, about what they would have to say or do, and some had wondered whether their birth parents would be present.

The children remembered with pleasure the special arrangements that had been made for their arrival; a newly decorated bedroom, presents or a celebratory meal. Most found their new parents reassuring and comforting, although they were sometimes confused about who was who in larger households or gatherings. Whilst arrival did not immediately dispel anxieties it did tend to modify them. Children had not always known how to fit into the routine of the house; the food could be strange and off-putting; the smells unfamiliar. They found some families more noisy, quieter, larger or smaller than those to which they were accustomed. So much was strange, even for those who had made prior visits. What was expected of them *now*? How should they behave? What would be happening next?

For many what happened next was going to a new school, and not necessarily at the beginning of a new year or even a new term. If anything, this created more apprehension than the prospect of a new family, although for some of the children of minority ethnic origin in the Thoburn study who had previously been living in 'white' areas, the pleasure of going to a new school where there were black or Asian pupils and teachers provided a strong counterbalance. A few children had visited the school beforehand; but, even for them, the lack of established friends as well as the fear of being teased or bullied conspired to create great anxiety. These are feelings that most of us can remember on joining a new school; but for these children such natural anxieties were compounded by those accompanying the upheaval of placement.

The enormous changes and adjustments that they had had to face over a short period were vividly recalled by the children. As one boy put it: 'I had to meet new family. Meet new houses. Meet new school. Everything really. Meet a new world'. What he and others described provides compelling evidence that children need to be as well prepared for such transitions as possible, whether they be to adoptive homes, foster homes or residential units.

The Main Points

The prospect of adoption by strangers creates anxiety and sometimes fear. This must be recognised and pains taken to provide reassurance.

Although necessary, reassurance and explanation are insufficient. Children also need to be given as much information as possible about what is in prospect. Visual material is likely to be particularly welcome.

Children should be given the opportunity (with help) to tell the adopters beforehand about themselves and their wishes in their own terms and with the aid of such things as tapes and videos.

First meetings are fraught affairs and create considerable anxiety. Children need to be well prepared and the arrangements sensitively managed.

Children ought to be clear about the purpose of meetings and visits and about what might be expected of them. In particular, they need to know whether they foreshadow a definite move or are by way of a 'try-out'.

Waiting for the final move can create uncertainty and more anxiety; but hasty moves can upset children as well. It is important to recognise that they need to do their own preparation and at their own pace – albeit with help where necessary.

Children cannot be detached from their pasts. They need to retain as many of the links with the people and things that are important to them as possible, especially in the period of transition. They should always be able to bring possessions with them, especially those that offer particular comfort.

Careful consideration needs to be given to when and if a child changes or starts school. The double change of home and school might be made easier were it to be staggered: for example, by placements being made in the holidays. When they do go to a new school careful preparation should have been made, not least by the school itself.

The preparation of the children who are to be placed

Much of the preparatory work that social workers did with the children appeared to revolve around life-story work. Virtually all the agencies replying to the Lowe and Murch questionnaire referred to it and two-thirds of the adopters said that their children had been involved in making such a record. The question arises, however, as to whether life-story work was regarded as a specific means of preparing children for placement or whether it was being used because it had already been started. In this respect it was notable that, whereas the children's concerns were mainly about the future (what was going to happen), the social workers tended to describe their preparatory work as helping children to deal with past trauma or painful emotions, mostly relying upon the spoken word rather than other techniques. Clearly, a child's preparation requires a variety of approaches. In the Quinton and Rushton study, for example, a psychologist or psychotherapist had been involved at some time in a third of the cases (primarily where children had been physically or sexually abused but usually only involving a single assessment meeting); but in only five cases had the preparatory work been undertaken by them.[1]

Different children will need different kinds of preparation and that implies that these needs will require to be assessed. It also means that preparation will take different amounts of time and involve different contributions. Furthermore, there is the question of the child's capacity to participate in these efforts. For example, Quinton and Rushton suggest that even high-quality work may have little beneficial effect when children are over-active or restless and unable to remain calm and to concentrate.

Some of the adopters were glowing in their praise of what had been done to prepare their child for the placement; others described quite inadequate or ineffective practice. The voluntary agencies in the Lowe and Murch study also

---

1 However, no analysis was undertaken of whether the involvement of a psychologist or a psychiatrist in the child's preparation made any difference to the outcomes.

criticised the preparation of some of the children referred to them and several of the local authorities acknowledged their inability to provide a high standard in all cases, usually because of the pressure of other activities or the lack of appropriately trained and experienced staff.

However, from what the adopters said it was apparent that they attached a good deal of importance to the role that foster carers had played in their child's preparation. Generally, they were described as sensitive and helpful, although there were instances where they had failed to prepare the child or where what they did was counter-productive. The contribution of foster carers or residential staff to a child's preparation has to be recognised and integrated with what is being done by social workers and others.

Although the provision of information and reassurance are essential parts of preparation, some children will require more than that. This may involve treatments of various kinds, some of which will need to be continued after the placement has been made. However, despite the studies in the Department of Health programme, we still know little about what is actually done or what requires to be done for different children. Nor is it clear how far preparation for adoption differs from the preparation that is needed for other major changes in the lives of vulnerable children, or, indeed (with regard to therapy, for example) from what ought to be being done anyway.

The Main Points
Certain basic preparation needs to be done with all children and in ways which they can understand. Beyond that the particular needs of each child should determine what is provided.
There may be a danger that because it is already done, or is in train, life-story work becomes a convenient vehicle for a child's preparation. It may not be enough.
Foster carers are important people in a child's preparation, capable of both facilitating and impeding a successful transition. They themselves need to be prepared if they are to prepare the child well.
There is a need for more detailed information about what is currently done by way of preparation, and also about how it relates to other ongoing direct work with the children.

Preparing other children

The preparation of other children for the subject child's adoption is clearly an important matter with respect to those children who are already established in the adoptive home. Over and above this there may be other children who should be prepared; for example, brothers or sisters from whom the child is separated or close friends. The preparation of such other children is likely to be different from that required by the child to be placed; but it should not be ignored.

The Rushton and Dance siblings study paid particular attention to the impact of an incoming child on the children already present. The new parents were asked how each of their birth children had reacted to the prospect of another child joining them. Half were said to have been keen on the idea but a third to have had reservations. They could wonder about whether they would like the new child; about how life would change, and about what they would have to give up or share. Nor was it only children of around the age of the child to be placed who could feel uncertain; some of those approaching adulthood who were still living at home had been hostile to the prospect of an addition to the family. Although most of the birth children who had left home accepted the plan, there were some who had worried about what their parents were taking on.

More than half (55%) of the adopters in the Quinton and Rushton study who already had children at home said that the family social workers had had a considerable amount of discussion with these children, but for the rest it had been minimal. Even so, there were no clues as to how the social workers – the children's social workers in particular – were assessing what the relationships between the in-coming and the established children might be. Nor was there any indication of how these relations were considered likely to affect the parents.

Of course, it can be presumed that all parents will take some steps to prepare the children already living with them for the impending adoption. Owen, for example, found that not only had previously adopted children been involved in the preliminary deliberations, but that where they had been party to the decision for another adopted child to join them no major difficulties had arisen as a result of sibling conflict. On the other hand, a few of the adopters in her study said that although they had wished to adopt a further child they had not done so because they had feared that it would be detrimental to the interests of the child or children they already had. We do not know how many prospective adopters abandon the idea for this reason or how many go ahead even when they, or the social worker, fear that the well-being of the established children could be threatened.

> **The Main Points**
>
> Other children who have been, or will become, a part of the placed child's life
>   need to be prepared for the impending adoption.
> The opposition of established children to the prospect of an adopted arrival may
>   be one reason why their parents decide not to proceed, as may their
>   calculation that such a step would have a deleterious effect on the children
>   they already have. We do not know. Nor do we know from these researches
>   how often social workers do or should advise against a placement for such
>   reasons.

The general preparation of the adopters

Introductory group meetings

One of the challenges in finding an appropriate way of introducing applicants
to the reality of adoption is that now, more than in the past, many of them will
not be first-time parents or first-time adopters. Half of those in the Lowe and
Murch postal sample and 60% of those in the Quinton and Rushton study had
birth children, and many in both groups had been or were foster carers or had
already adopted. Nearly three-quarters of those in the first of these studies had
some parenting experience and over 80% in the second. This is a radical
change from the past and has to be taken into account in the kind of
preparation offered. Indeed, it was those who regarded themselves as
experienced parents who were most critical of the meetings organised by way
of preliminary preparation. It may also be this group who need help to
recognise the differences between raising a birth child and caring for an older
child by adoption.

Even so, 42% of those in the Quinton and Rushton sample said that they
had benefited very much from these meetings and the same proportion felt that
they had gained something from attending. However, what was most
appreciated by those in both this and the Lowe and Murch study was the
chance to hear from and talk to people who had already had children placed
with them. Moreover, both the experienced and inexperienced alike usually
recognised that the meetings provided an opportunity to consider the number
of children they might take and the particular problems that might arise in the
adoption of an older child. Many also acknowledged that the meetings had
helped them to reflect upon their own strengths and weaknesses. Two of the
specific criticisms however were that insufficient attention had been paid to the

impact of adoption on birth children and that undue emphasis had been placed upon 'challenging behaviour' and other possible difficulties without a balancing discussion of the satisfactions that adoption could bring.

Owen also noted that the general preparation of single adopters may need to be slanted somewhat differently from that intended for couples. Some of the single adopters had found the group meetings arranged and conducted as if all those present were couples. In particular, when sessions were believed to involve assessment as well as preparation, single people felt that the questions and comments probed more deeply into their circumstances than those of the married couples; for example, questions about what child care arrangements would be made by those who were in employment. Some of the black adopters also said that they would have appreciated the presence of black staff.

Thus, although the majority of adopters had found the introductory group meetings helpful in one respect or another, there was a minority (perhaps one in seven) who had not, whilst others had specific criticisms. There was no information about the opinions of those who withdrew at this stage or who were not subsequently approved. The meetings could have provided enough information for them to decide not to proceed, or they might have been alienated by the process. We do not know. Certainly, some of those in the Owen study who eventually adopted reported that they had felt uncomfortable in the group settings, being unaccustomed to such situations and anxious about speaking in public. However, it needs to be noted that whereas 82% of those in the Lowe and Murch postal survey who were approved by voluntary agencies found the preparation groups a helpful source of information, this proportion fell to 53% in the case of those approved by statutory agencies. This suggests that there may have been differences in the manner in which these occasions were organised. It is also noteworthy that whilst most agencies required or expected attendance, there were some that made it optional.

Preparing themselves

The preparation provided by the agencies is only part of the story. Prospective adopters make their own preparations, often starting well before their first enquiries. For example, half of those in the Lowe and Murch study said that they had drawn upon information or advice from family and friends and about 40% that they had gathered preparatory material or sought guidance from others who had adopted or who were intending to do so. Half had also consulted books, read pamphlets or watched introductory videos.

However, friends or neighbours may give wrong information or perpetuate mistaken beliefs. For example, some of the single adopters in the Owen sample had thought that the adoption regulations were more rigid than they actually were; for instance with respect to religion, marital status, or income. Likewise, some of the black adopters had felt that different standards would be applied to them than to white adopters. There are almost certainly still false assumptions about the nature and process of adoption that deter some people from taking the first steps.

However, once they had approached an agency it was common practice for enquirers to be sent an information pack, sometimes with a questionnaire which they could choose to complete or not; but even at this stage some people felt that their suitability was already starting to be assessed.

Preparation or assessment?

The convergence of these two processes was likely to become more pronounced as further steps were taken. Even though the majority (68%) of the adopters responding to the postal questionnaire in the Lowe and Murch study said that preliminary interviews with social workers had provided them with useful information, many still felt that these occasions had been used as opportunities to vet them, as indeed was often the case. This may make prospective adopters defensive and distort both preparation and assessment. It certainly seems plausible that 'preparation as learning' could be compromised when interviews or group meetings are experienced as inquisitorial, although it is difficult to see how this could be avoided altogether. Even so, it should be made clear to prospective adopters whether or not these early meetings do include an element of assessment. Certainly, as far as the group meetings were concerned, most agencies said that they did.

The Main Points
One of the dramatic changes in adoption is that many prospective adopters have already had experience of parenting. This calls for a careful consideration of the kinds of preliminary preparation that are needed, as does the fact that more will be single people and from minority ethnic backgrounds.
Adopters derive considerable value from the opportunity to talk to others who are also involved in considering an application, and especially those with prior experience. More might be done in the early stages to bring previous adopters into the preparatory groups.

It needs to be made clear whether or not the preparatory introductions are also
opportunities for agencies to start the process of assessment. Even then, it
should be recognised that where assessment accompanies preparation it may
impede people's learning or their willingness to raise issues that they believe
reflect badly on their suitability to adopt.

Adopters take steps to prepare themselves; they are not the passive recipients of
what agencies offer. This may lead to or confirm misconceptions that deter
people from making an enquiry, let alone an application. Misleading hearsay
needs to be combated by the systematic provision of easily available and
accurate information.

The specific preparation of the adopters

Once a particular child has been 'matched' with them, the preparation of the
adopters takes on a different complexion and gives rise to somewhat different
issues. The relevant studies cover three main features: the provision of
information; the arrangements for introductions, further meetings and visits;
and preparation for the court hearing.

Information

Adopters wanted as much information as possible about the child to be placed
with them. Much of what was provided appeared to be conveyed orally. For
example, two-fifths of those responding to the Lowe and Murch postal survey
said that information about their child's emotional needs had only been
provided in this way, and a third that this was also true with respect to their
child's religious background. It was most common, however, for information to
be given both orally and in writing, although the authors conclude that more
should have been written down in order to help parents absorb, reflect upon
and understand what they had been told and, one might add, to enable
agencies to keep a proper record.

The postal questionnaire also asked adopters whether or not they had
received information about eleven items. Ninety per cent or more had been told
about their children's medical, educational, ethnic and care backgrounds as
well as their emotional needs and birth family history. A similar proportion had
been given some legal information. Around 80% had been provided with
information about the impact that the child's past was likely to have on their
behaviour, about their religion, their cultural or 'other' background details.

Some three-quarters thought that the information which they had received had been clear and almost 80% had found it helpful. However, only half considered it to have been sufficient or up-to-date. In a few cases adopters considered that some facts had been deliberately withheld or distorted. Without accurate and honest information adopters are handicapped in preparing themselves or others (such as the school) for their child's arrival. In this respect it is of interest that a third of the families said that they had been allowed to see the agency's file on their child.

Only 34% of the new parents in the Quinton and Rushton study had been fully content with the medical information about the child that they had been given; 54% had found it deficient in certain respects (especially in relation to matters of mental health and genetic risks), and 12% claimed not to have had any medical information at all. Of those who had wanted more, two-thirds said that they had been frustrated in their attempts to obtain it. Rather more (56%) had been satisfied with the information that had been provided about their child's background. Of those who had found it inadequate or incorrect 40% had pressed for more, two-thirds of them successfully. Many found the life-story books a valuable source of information about the child's past. A little over a half (55%) of the parents had been given extensive information about their child's emotional and behavioural profile. (Where they were provided, videos were much appreciated.) The remaining parents said that they had received few, if any, facts about these matters, especially when the placements had been hurried. Again, some felt that they had actually been misinformed – with emotional and behavioural problems either having been exaggerated or played down. Forty-four per cent of the parents said that they had been given a considerable amount of information about their child's daily routines. However, a fifth claimed to have received no guidance on the matter and the other third only a little. Some contacted previous carers in order to fill the gaps.

Taken together, however, only 12% of the respondents in the Quinton and Rushton study were satisfied with the information they had received in all four of these areas. A half said that it was deficient on one or two counts and 37% that it was inadequate on three or four.

The crucial importance to the adopters of having information about a child's background was exemplified in the Owen study. All the children had 'special needs'.[2] Almost half had serious learning difficulties; a third were known to have been sexually abused; one was blind, many had hearing or speech

---

2 However, these 'special needs' included those for the child to have an ethnically or racially 'matched' placement.

impediments, whilst there were those who suffered from epilepsy, chronic infections or febrile convulsions. Nearly a fifth had Down's syndrome and, overall, a fifth were mentally or physically disabled, or both. Obviously, these conditions overlapped, but the list does convey the imperative need for adopters to have full and accurate information, first in order to know 'what they are taking on' and, secondly, in order to plan their child's care. In that respect it was encouraging that the medical problems of the children in this study were said usually to have been well documented; but this may have been because they were so prominent. Information about emotional and behavioural problems had been less complete.

The Thoburn team make a different point concerning the negative nature of the information on file about the birth parents, information which was often passed on to the adoption panels and to the adopters. Not only could it be negative but sometimes racist in tone. This was likely to have given black adopters an unfavourable impression of the agency and made it difficult for white adopters to promote a positive ethnic identity in their black or mixed-parentage children.

The adopters in the Romanian study received very little preparatory help from social workers, but there is likely to be a need for those intending to adopt from overseas to receive help in appreciating issues concerning heritage and identity; and this would be true in the case of others who are adopting children of a different ethnic or religious background to themselves.

Introductions

Most of the introductions took place in foster homes and a few in residential establishments; but whatever the location they were accompanied by a fair degree of formality. These first encounters were emotionally charged – for the child and the adopters alike. The accounts which the adopters gave of these meetings were both detailed and vivid. They worried about who would be in the room first; about how long they would have to wait; but, above all, whether they and the child would like each other. Most of the adopters had seen a photograph of the child beforehand, but it was not clear whether the children had had the same advantage.

In some cases the introductions had occurred immediately after the children had returned from school when, presumably, they were tired. On other occasions there were numerous people present, which adopters criticised and which must have been confusing for the child. Since these meetings were usually held in their homes foster carers were normally present, some, according to the adopters in the Lowe and Murch study, proving to have been extremely supportive and others not. However, whatever the climate of the meeting it could be difficult for the children because of feelings of split loyalties. Certainly, adopters were disconcerted when they were at once introduced as the child's future mum and dad. Others were surprised when the child addressed them as such. When this happened the preparation of the adopters, the child and the foster carers was unlikely to have been harmonised, most notably with respect to the purpose of the introduction.

The next step after the first meeting was usually for the children to be visited again by the adopters (and often taken out) and then for them to make visits to the adopters' home. A third of the children in the Quinton and Rushton sample were placed within a month of the first meeting; most (43%) between one and three months afterwards, and only 17% more slowly than that. The majority (70%) of the adoptive parents were satisfied with the length of the introductory period; of the rest two-thirds felt that it had been too drawn-out whilst the remaining third thought that it had been too short. Whatever the most appropriate tempo it seems unlikely that rapid placements can provide sufficient opportunity for what might be regarded as 'transitional preparation', either for the child or the adopters.

Lowe and Murch also commented on the length of the introductory period. Some of those whom they interviewed 'wanted to get on with it' and were frustrated by what they regarded as unnecessary delay. However, there were others who had found the pace too rushed. The preliminary visits were also felt to have been inadequate when their intended length was cut short, usually because of pressure from the foster carers. Indeed, some of the interviewees highlighted the considerable influence that the foster carers had had upon all aspects of the introductory period. Those who had wanted to adopt the child themselves, to keep them as foster children, or who had disapproved of the adopters could make visits to their homes difficult and tense occasions. On the other hand, there were those who were anxious for the children to leave, pressing social workers to hurry along the placement and to that end, it was said, sometimes giving misleading or incomplete information about the child. In between these extremes there were those who made the visits as easy as possible and who fully accepted the proposed timetable.

It should be noted that several of the interviewees in the Lowe and Murch study gave disturbing accounts of the problems that arose when they returned children to their foster homes after their visits. Although reactions will differ as between different children and the different circumstances it is clear from these accounts that careful preparation is needed for the transitional coming and going.

Lowe and Murch also described the reactions of the adopters to meeting birth parents (usually the mother) during the period of introductions and visits. Most of the adopters who had done so before the placement described it in positive terms, although also finding it a highly charged occasion. Many saw it as helpful for answering children's questions later on, for being better placed to appreciate what they might say or feel, and for obtaining additional information. However, there were some who viewed such meetings as having been entirely negative, whilst there were also examples of those who had refused to meet birth parents, finding the prospect too emotionally daunting. Even so, almost all of the agencies said that they encouraged such meetings (at which times agreements for contact were sometimes signed).

Preparing for the hearing

Once the placement had been made the idea of preparation was largely superseded by that of support. However, as the Lowe and Murch interviews made plain, the adopters may have needed more preparation for the court hearing than they had received. A great deal of anxiety was reported about what might or might not happen, especially where there was more than one hearing. What would they have to do and say? Would they come face-to-face with the birth parents? What were the likely ramifications when the case was contested? Would the order be granted? There was, indeed, a remarkable similarity between these apprehensions and those described by the children. Just as the children needed to be prepared for what many of them saw as a forthcoming ordeal, so did the adopters. Some who had engaged a solicitor and were represented (mainly when the case was contested) looked to them for guidance, although there were instances where adopters felt that they had been falsely assured that all would be plain sailing or where they had been needlessly worried about difficulties that were actually unlikely to arise.[3]

Better preparation for going to court might well have reduced adopters' anxieties, as would have been being kept abreast of what progress the preparations for the hearing had made and what the timetable was likely to be. Furthermore, they also needed to be prepared for a postponement or

3 This may reflect the observations in both this and the *Pathways* study that the lawyers dealing with adoption cases were not always experienced in this area.

adjournment where this was likely since when these came as a surprise they were clearly very unsettling.

The Main Points
Adopters must receive full and accurate information about the child they are intending to adopt and it should usually be written down. The studies point to clear deficiencies, although these may reflect the difficulties confronting social workers in obtaining what is required.
As well as the child, both adopters and foster carers need to be helped to prepare for first meetings. They are difficult and anxious occasions. Social workers need to plan ahead.
The purpose of introductory and subsequent meetings or visits needs to be made clear to everybody involved. In particular, it should be decided beforehand whether they mark the beginning of a definite linkage or whether they remain exploratory. The children and the adopters should not have different expectations.
The appropriate pace and duration of the interim visits need to be assessed carefully in each case.
Foster parents play an important part in determining the period over which the introductory visits are spread. They need to be taken into account in planning this stage of the preparation.
Without adequate preparation the child's coming and going between their old and their new home in the transitional period can be a stressful process.
The prospect of the court hearing creates anxiety for both adopters and children. Their careful and realistic preparation by both social workers and solicitors should not be overlooked.
Although none of the studies addressed, except incidentally, the issue of the preparation of the birth parents or other members of the birth family their needs should not be ignored.

Selection

What the children had to say

Although older children often remembered being consulted about the *idea* of being adopted and being asked whether they wanted to be adopted by the people with whom they had been placed, far fewer recalled being asked what kind of adopters or adoptive family they would like to join. However, 17 of the 41 children in the Thomas and Beckford study were able to describe the type of family for which they had hoped. Five had wished that there would be other children and one that they would be an only child. Five more had wanted to be placed with all or some of their birth siblings (although, in the event only four were); another had definitely not wanted to be with her four siblings and was glad that it did not happen. For one girl what was important was that there should be a dog. It was not clear, however, how far the children had been encouraged to tell those responsible for arranging their adoption what they had in mind; indeed in the Thoburn study it was noted that the information on file about the child's wishes was sparse. Nevertheless, there was a record of nine not having wished to move from their current placement and of 11 who wanted to go back to their parents or relatives. There were also instances of children wishing to be adopted by their foster carers but who were placed elsewhere instead.

However, in general, what children had wanted were parents who were 'nice', 'kind', 'funny' and 'normal'. An 11 year-old girl in the Thomas and Beckford study had wanted: 'somebody to look after me if I'm hurt and sad and someone who will play with me'. Her sister (8) had wanted 'a family that would take care of me and not leave me alone. And when I want them they always come. And feed me properly, and look after me, and be kind ...'. A 12 year-old boy explained that he wanted a new family that would help him and his sister get over their difficult past experiences. Another wanted a mother and father 'who didn't smack', whilst one of those in the Thoburn sample emphasised that he 'wouldn't have gone to any family ... I would want to make sure they treated us right'. Hopes like these were likely to have reflected past neglect or ill-treatment. Not only did such children want to avoid a repetition of what had befallen them, but some also looked for parents who would 'make things better', heal some of the past hurt or put things right. For some black children who had been living in a white foster home this meant going to a black family: one such child 'knew it wasn't right that we were living in a white home ...'.

Having been told that they were to be adopted, many of the children in the Thomas and Beckford study then had to wait whilst a suitable family was found. It was often difficult for most to remember just how long that had been, but for those who did it was generally 'too long', 'ages' or 'five years'. More importantly, however, the children described how it felt to have to wait. One of the consequences of a lengthy interval was a growing sense of not being wanted, particularly when they knew that they had been advertised without success. As one girl remembered: 'it didn't feel very nice, that you weren't being chosen'. Conversely, those who knew that many families had responded to 'their' advertisement felt valued. Even so, it should be borne in mind that children do see these advertisements and can be upset and angry (as some were) about unflattering descriptions or, in their view, inaccurate statements.

There were only a few reports in the Owen study of instances where children had been asked in advance what kind of family they would like to join. However, where this happened it proved to be a good way of involving them in the decision. A few of the girls had hoped that there would not be a 'dad' in the family.

One way in which a small number of the children in the Thomas and Beckford study remembered being involved in the selection of their new family was through making what amounted to an exploratory visit. As one boy explained: 'first we came here and had a look and then we went back and chatted to the social worker. And we said, "yes, we'd like to go there ...". So then we went here. Packed all the bags and came. We were adopted.' However, for most children their preliminary meetings with the adoptive family were either somewhat confusing or were understood as a way for them to get to know those who had been chosen for them.

The Main Points

If the requirements of the Children Act 1989 that children's views about their placement should be elicited and taken into account are to be observed, the question of children's preferences for the *kind* of family which they might join cannot be ignored, although they may not always be able to be met or may not always be considered to be wise.

Children have views about the kinds of parents they would like to have: primarily, people who will care for them in a kindly and committed fashion. They are also able to say what they do *not* want; for example, parents who smack, leave them alone or who are white when they are black.

> For children to be told that they are to be adopted and then, apparently, not chosen for a long time is likely to reinforce any sense of unworthiness. This raises the question of when the prospect of adoption is best broached with them.
> Children should be given the opportunity to say no to a proposed placement. This will require specific preparation.

The selection and approval of adopters

Motives

Owen makes the point that most of the adopters in her study had been considering the possibility of adoption well before making an enquiry, let alone a formal application. Both she and several of the other researchers note the importance of certain triggers that start the process going: newspaper articles, television programmes, certain discussions or meetings. If agencies are to mount effective recruitment campaigns they need to understand who would consider adopting as well as what converts that disposition into action.

Most of the studies emphasise how diverse motives can now be; but, broadly speaking, they suggest that there are those which revolve around infertility and those which might be termed 'altruistic'. Whereas infertility was a major reason for adopting in the past it is less so today. Many adopters of older children already have birth children. However, it should not be concluded that infertility only provides the motivation to adopt for a minority. In the first place, as the BAAF *Focus on Adoption* study indicates, once younger children are included the proportion of adopters who do not have birth children is considerably greater (73%). Secondly, infertility may still be a common reason for *wanting* to adopt, especially babies, but not necessarily a principal reason amongst those who eventually *do* adopt. Thirdly, some of those who have had children born to them may be unable or unwilling to have any more, but still wish to enlarge their family. Finally, there are single adopters (and indeed some couples) who are not infertile but who are nevertheless childless.

Despite its decline in relative importance, therefore, infertility remains an important motive to adopt and, as interviewees in several of the studies were at pains to stress, the process of being questioned about it is experienced as particularly unwelcome. Most respondents said that they understood why it was necessary; but they wanted it done with sensitivity and only once. Those who were questioned about the matter on several occasions, and by different people, resented it; for example, when they were adopting a second or subsequent child and had, therefore, already been through an investigation.

Other motives for seeking to adopt, although often grouped together as 'altruistic', were varied. There were, for example, those who adopted children who were already known to them or for whom they were already caring. The studies suggest that this group may be larger than is commonly assumed. Thirty-four per cent of those who were interviewed in the Lowe and Murch research had been the child's foster carers. (BAAF has estimated that in 1996 a quarter of all adopters of children from care were their foster carers.[1]) In both Owen's and Thoburn's studies there were also examples of people adopting the children of relatives; children whom they had encountered in a professional capacity, and the children of friends. In the *Pathways* study 7% of *all* adoptions were by relatives other than step parents. Such links may not be frequent but they add to the number of children who are already known to those who adopt them.

Many adopters in several of the studies certainly explained their reasons for having wanted to adopt in altruistic terms, reflecting a mixture of compassion, sympathy, the desire to make a social contribution and the conviction that they had something to give. A quarter of the adopters in the Owen study referred to their religious beliefs in explaining what had moved them to adopt. Specifically wanting to provide a home for a black child was an important part of the motivation of African-Caribbean parents in the Thoburn study.

Nonetheless, most of those who were interviewed acknowledged that they had seen adoption as meeting a mixture of their own needs and those of a child. This was borne out in the study of parental satisfaction amongst adopters of the Romanian children who were under two when they joined their new families. Although most (78%) of the mothers said that infertility was their main reason for wanting to adopt, many explained their motives in altruistic terms as well. It was noteworthy that those who gave both infertility and altruism as major reasons for having adopted were significantly less likely than either of the other two groups (in which either infertility or altruism was the main consideration) to report negative evaluations of the adoption. It was also notable that in the control group of domestic adoptions of children under six months, 96% of the parents gave infertility as the sole reason for their decision.

Of course, these data provide only a glimpse of the motives that people have for wanting to adopt; but Lowe and Murch also asked what it was that led

1 BAAF (1998), *Children Adopted from Care: an Examination of Agency Adoptions in England – 1996.*

people to adopt an *older* child. One factor was that he or she was already known to them; another was that they had not wanted to be involved in the kinds of intimate care that infants require. However, there were others who had wanted a baby or infant but who had agreed to take an older child because that was all that was proposed; in this sense there was a measure of disappointment. As one said, 'we would have adopted a Romanian child [an infant] had we been able to afford it'. There were also those who had wished to adopt an older child but not as old as the one with whom they had been 'matched'. Lowe and Murch warn that particular caution should be exercised in persuading people to take an older child than they had envisaged.

The importance of 'motivation' lies in the fact that it is closely related to the expectations that adopters hold of the adoption; to the nature of their commitment, and to the satisfactions or disappointments that the adoption brings. It is also an important consideration in the design and focus of any recruitment programme.

Agency policies and practices

Lowe and Murch asked the agencies what selection policies they operated. They also asked the adopters what policies they had encountered. Some agencies had policies that excluded or deterred certain applicants in the early stages; for example, by imposing upper age limits (especially for baby adoptions). Some adopters said that they had been confronted with other conditions, such as the requirement that wives should give up their full-time work or that couples should not continue with IVF treatment. Others reported that, as foster carers, they had felt that their application was frowned upon, although no agency actually stated that they had a policy against them adopting.

The adopters who gave these accounts of their experiences had, it should be borne in mind, eventually adopted. We do not know how many applicants were rejected or deterred by the preconditions that may have been imposed. Nor do we know what precisely these criteria were, or how widely they were applied. There were certainly closed lists for baby adoptions and thus the possibility that those who insisted on having a baby would be ruled out from the start. Others (an unknown number) will have been screened out, or will have decided not to proceed once they had learnt more about what was involved. One agency in the Lowe and Murch research estimated that there was a 75% rate of attrition between first enquiries and taking up statutory references.

Approvals

Thus, many applicants, or potential applicants, will have fallen by the wayside before their names reached an adoption panel for consideration. None of the studies tells us much about this stage of the process, and we do not know what proportion of candidates for approval were rejected. Lowe and Murch found that some of those whom they interviewed had had a previous application rejected by a panel before having been successful later. These people described the hurt, embarrassment and anger that they felt, as well as the fear that it would be thought that they had been unacceptable for sinister reasons, such as child abuse or criminal activities. These feelings remained despite the fact that most of them had had the grounds for their rejection explained and, in a few cases, had been given the opportunity to appeal and/or to attend a post-rejection meeting. However, few if any of the adopters had been permitted to be present when the panel discussed their application (5% of the statutory cases and 15% of the voluntary).

One of the other issues which the Owen study in particular illuminated is what might be called 'the hierarchy of eligibility'. It was clear from her study of single-person adoptions that these placements had often been regarded by the referring agencies as options of last resort when, often after considerable searching, a suitable *couple* could not be found. The same feeling of only having been approved as a last resort was expressed by some of the foster-carer adopters in the Lowe and Murch study.

The Main Points

It is important to understand and then to minimise the misunderstandings, anxieties or deterrents that prevent potential adopters from coming forward. Equally, the triggers that encourage those who are contemplating adoption to make the first move need to be appreciated. Without such understanding, otherwise suitable adopters may fail to be recruited.

The adoption of 'known' children should not be overlooked, in particular the adoption of foster children. It seems sensible to approve applications where foster placements have become *de facto* adoptions, particularly where that is what the child wants.

It needs to be recognised that as the age of the children being adopted has increased so have the reasons for wanting to adopt. However, infertility remains important amongst them and this requires particularly sensitive handling in the necessary investigations.

The small number of babies and infants needing adoption may lead some applicants to accept (or be persuaded to accept) an older child than they had in mind. This may build in inevitable disappointment and disillusionment.

Any eligibility criteria operated by agencies need to be reviewed from time to time in the light of changing social patterns and children's needs.

Applicants who are rejected find the experience hurtful and fear that others will assume that they are unfit for discreditable reasons. 'Post-rejection' help should be available.

Matching children and adopters

The waiting period

The time between their approval and a firm linkage was reported by many of the adopters as a difficult and frustrating period. Some relied upon the agencies to find a suitable child, others took steps to do so for themselves. Either way there could be a long wait, although sometimes adopters were taken by surprise at the speed with which a proposal was made. It was important to them to be kept informed of what was happening. They felt isolated and forgotten when they heard nothing from the agencies. It is important to know how many drop out as a result, although none of the studies provided such information.

Saying yes, or saying no

Drawing upon what she was told by the adopters in her study Owen characterised the next stage, when a child is proposed, as one of bargaining and negotiation. The adopters felt caught up in a competition. For example, they might hear rumours from their network that it was hard to get a girl or children of a certain age, and thus consider themselves to be under some pressure to say 'yes'.

Such pressure, as Lowe and Murch found, could be especially strongly felt when adopters had been waiting a long time; when they were aware that others were also being considered for the same child, or when they were unsure what would happen if they decided that a particular child was not the one for them. When adopters have had to wait a long time they may be so relieved when a child is proposed that even if they have doubts these may be overridden by their anxiety to adopt. Not only may adopters feel under pressure to say 'yes' for reasons like these but also because an initial meeting with the child has been so conducted that they feel they cannot back out; for example, when they are introduced from the outset as the child's future mum and dad. The question arises, therefore, of how realistically the option of saying 'no' to a proposed linkage is presented and how clearly any implications of doing so are spelled out (that, for example, those who do will continue to be considered for other children).

Against this background it was interesting that Lowe and Murch also endeavoured to discover why those who *had* said 'no' on a previous occasion had done so. One prominent reason was because they had decided that the placement of a particular child would not fit in with their birth children or would have affected them detrimentally.

The social workers interviewed in the Lowe and Murch study described similar dilemmas to those faced by some of the prospective adopters. If a child had been waiting a long time for an adoptive family they might go ahead with a placement despite certain misgivings. In other cases they reported feeling that they had to do so because of pressure from foster carers who wanted a child moved or because of directives that more children should be adopted.

The components of the matching assessments

Both the Rushton and Dance and the Quinton and Rushton studies provided additional information about which children went to which families; for example, that children placed alone apart from their siblings were more likely to enter established families and that sibling groups more often went to those without children. There was also, for instance, a trend for those children in the Quinton and Rushton sample who had had most moves in their care careers to be placed with older carers; and this was also true for those who had experienced most unplanned moves and who had returned home most often. It has also been noted that a large proportion of the children placed with the single adopters in the Owen study were disabled. How far such patterns reflected *general* assumptions about which kinds of children should be placed with which types of families is unclear. Indeed, the categories into which each are divided remain rudimentary; for example, in the case of the children, the division between those who have been sexually abused and those who have not, or that between those who have been rejected by their birth families and those who have not. Different categories are assumed to imply different needs: the needs themselves (apart from the need for a permanent family) would still seem to be largely unclassified.[2] That is not to say that they were not carefully

---

2 See, however, Dartington Social Research Unit (nd), *Matching Needs and Services: the Audit and Planning of Provision for Children Looked After by Local Authorities.*

assessed, only that there was comparatively little evidence from these studies about what was taken into account in reaching particular conclusions.

However, Lowe and Murch suggested seven groups of factors that appeared to have determined the linkages that were made in their study. These were: geography (important in terms of whether or not contact was envisaged); urgency (significant when there was pressure to avoid delay); inter-agency arrangements (where agencies belonged to a consortium the range of placements was usually enlarged); the children's needs and wishes (although these were not always recorded and it was unclear how often and how far they were influential); the adopters' capacities and preferences (again, however, it was difficult to discern which factors exercised the most influence); the involvement of the birth parents (some agencies described two or three possible adopters to them and invited a choice); and ethnicity, religion, race, culture and language.

Ethnicity

Several important points concerning the linking of children from minority ethnic groups with adopters or foster carers emerged from the Thoburn team's study. Both the children and their new parents in 'same-race' placements believed that this policy should be followed if at all possible. Some of the children who had been placed trans-racially also argued strongly for a policy of ethnically matched placements, although most also acknowledged that they had learned much from their white parents. Children of mixed parentage appeared to feel less strongly about the issue. Of course, all these arrangements had been made in the early 1980s when the placement of black children with white families was more common. Indeed, in the cohort study (which comprised children from minority ethnic backgrounds (42%) or those of mixed parentage (58%)) both parents were white in 71% of the placements; 13% consisted of two African Caribbean parents; in 11% there was a mixed partnership, and in 2% both parents were of Asian origin. More up-to-date figures, such as those produced by BAAF for all children adopted from care in 1995, indicate that a much smaller proportion is now being placed trans-racially: 24% of the adoptions recorded by local authorities and 6% of those reported by voluntary agencies.[3]

---

3 BAAF (1997), *Focus on Adoption: a Snapshot of Adoption Patterns in England – 1995*. The report suggests 'that some of the trans-racial adoptions may be accounted for by white foster carers applying to adopt children of minority ethnic backgrounds who may have been with them for some years'.

Nonetheless, the Thoburn results provide a benchmark, as well as indicating some of the characteristics of trans-racial placements. First, they were more likely to have involved foster carers than adopters. Secondly, it was more common for younger children to be placed trans-racially. Thirdly, this was also the case for children of mixed parentage, 88% of whom had been placed with new parents who were white compared with 63% of those whose birth parents were both black. However, as Thoburn and her colleagues point out, the idea of 'ethnic matching' can suggest a closer similarity between the child and the new family than is in fact the case. For instance, although some of the children of direct African origin had been placed with black parents, in no instance were they both also from a direct African background. Children of south Asian parents were the most likely to have been placed with those of a similar background, perhaps because of religious considerations. The importance of such findings lies in what they suggest about the assumptions which lie behind decisions concerning the 'matching' of children and new parents. In this case the clearest of these was a greater willingness to place mixed-parentage than black children with white families and the belief that colour was a more significant consideration than race, ethnicity or culture, except possibly with respect to religion.

Some of the complexities of 'ethnic matching' are also exposed in the Quinton and Rushton research, although only one in six of the children in that sample had minority ethnic backgrounds. Half of them were 'ethnically matched'; but it was the descriptions of those who were not which illustrated some of the dilemmas faced by social workers. All except one were of mixed parentage, and all of these were more than one generation removed from their minority ethnic origins. The one African-Caribbean child who was placed trans-racially was placed together with a white sibling. Furthermore, many of these children had been born to white mothers and had grown up in a predominantly white culture.

A third of the children in the Owen study were black or of mixed parentage. All had been placed with black adopters except one whom the white adopter had known beforehand through family connections. The research suggested that the priority attached to racial or cultural matching by the three voluntary agencies concerned seemed to favour the choice of a single parent in some cases because a single black woman was seen as preferable to a white couple (although not necessarily to a black couple) and because such applicants were seen as having a high level of acceptability within the black community.

Almost all the agencies that replied to the Lowe and Murch postal questionnaire explained that ethnic or cultural matching was the preferred option but some two-fifths said that various circumstances could lead to a departure from that policy. It was notable, however, that the voluntary agencies were more likely than the local authorities to pursue unwavering 'same-race' policies (52% of them compared with 24% of the statutory bodies). Where second or third best options had to be found preferences tended to follow an order of diminishing connection with minority ethnic status; for example, from families where one of the adopters was black to those where the couple were of mixed parentage; then on to families where one of the partners had a mixed background, and finally to a white family, but one living in a multi-cultural community.

This last option draws attention to the extent to which efforts are or are not made to place minority ethnic children in areas where they will have the opportunity to mix with others of a similar background, at school, in clubs or simply in the neighbourhood. The importance of this was stressed by the black children in the Owen study and by those in the Thoburn research. However, the extent to which such considerations affected the selection of a particular family for a child was not explored in any of the studies, nor was the question of whether this only became a serious consideration if an 'ideal' ethnic 'match' proved impossible to achieve.

The Main Points

Once they have been approved, adopters need to be kept well informed about the progress being made towards a placement.

Placements that are made under a measure of duress and against the better judgement of adopters are best avoided. It must be made clear to them that there *is* a choice and that a refusal does not rule them out.

The needs and the wishes of the children must be taken into account in deciding upon suitable adopters; but if these needs are to be met as closely as possible they cannot be divorced from the capacities and expectations of prospective adopters.

Placements may give the impression of being ethnically matched when colour is treated as the pre-eminent consideration; but placements matched for colour are not necessarily matched for race or culture. The grounds for matching black with black may lie elsewhere than simply in ethnicity, most notably in the nurturing of a black identity and in defence against racism.

The large proportion of mixed-parentage children (particularly those brought up by white birth mothers) amongst those being adopted from care can create a dilemma for placement policy and practice. However, older children are likely to have a view about what should happen and this should be respected.

5

Contact[1]

What the children had to say

A recurring theme in the children's comments was the sense of loss at having to leave their birth families and, in certain cases, others (such as foster carers) to whom they had become attached. The person most often missed was the birth mother, much less often the birth father. Second to this the children missed birth siblings. As Owen points out: 'the sense of loss surrounding these previous family members was capable of remaining, even when there were other people in the adoptive family who were well-liked ...'. Similarly, Thoburn concluded from her discussions with the young people in her study that 'painful feelings about those experiences which led to their leaving their birth families never went away'. Despite such feelings of loss, particularly amongst the children who were older at placement, attitudes towards 'contact' were mixed and seemed to depend upon past experience, age at adoption and aspirations for the future. They were also related to the kind of contact involved; its frequency and with whom. There was, however, often a difference between the views of those who had contact and those who did not.

From what the children said it was clear that the functions that contacts fulfilled, or might fulfil, needed to be understood. These covered: the need for direct information; reassurance about the well-being of family members; the desire to enhance their sense of identity; and the wish, particularly amongst older children, to determine the place of their birth family in their future lives. Thus, it is not only important to establish a child's preferences about contact (which may change over time and with the experience of contact) but to appreciate the reasons for them.

The complexity of children's attitudes to contact was apparent in what they said they wanted. Amongst those in the Thomas and Beckford study who had contact with birth parents (mainly with mothers) about half were satisfied with the arrangements as they stood; the other half would have liked more contact.

---

1 For a review of the issues see Mullender A (ed) (1991), Open Adoption: the Philosophy and Practice, BAAF; and for a recent small-scale study Fratter J (1996), Adoption with Contact: Implications for Policy and Practice, BAAF.

Only one child wanted less. Of those who did not have such contact however, about half said that they were content with the way things were; a quarter were definite that they did not want any contact and another quarter that they did.

What Thoburn and her colleagues were told by those who had had no contact with their birth parents covered a range of feelings from 'not needing it, to curiosity, wistfulness [and] regret'. Furthermore, it was, they reported, harder for them than those with contact to resolve these feelings. It was also found that 'those who knew that a sibling had remained with a birth parent seemed particularly driven to re-establish contact'. Although the young people who had maintained contact with birth parents expressed both positive and negative views about the experience, they were more likely than those who had not to have a realistic picture of these parents' circumstances.

The reasons that children offered for *not* wanting contact with birth parents are important to consider. One was because they had been placed at a young age and did not remember the birth family or particular members of it; another was because they felt angry at what they regarded as their abandonment. Further reasons included anxiety or fear about what contact might entail and a sense of loyalty to the adoptive parents.

There was less variation in children's views with respect to contact with siblings from whom they had been separated, although many more *had* contact with siblings than with birth parents and of these none wanted less. However, the majority (four-fifths) of those in the Thomas and Beckford study who did not have contact were content with the prevailing arrangements. It should also be noted that some who wanted contact (or more contact) with siblings differentiated between them, especially between those whom they knew and those they did not.

Contact, however, extended beyond birth parents and siblings. Previous foster carers were important; indeed, a third of the children in the Thomas and Beckford study had such contact. Most of it was face-to-face, but telephone conversations were also valued. Some children treated previous foster carers as confidants, grandparents or counsellors: others had significant contacts with members of the extended birth family (mainly grandparents) and with former social workers.

The Main Points

Children's attitudes towards 'contact' are complex and far from uniform. They vary significantly according to whether or not it exists, by age, and by past experience. What contact children want or do not want should not be taken for granted; and it may well change.

Contact serves many purposes for the child and these should be understood and
may point to different types of contact and with different people.
Birth mothers and siblings are generally the most significant contacts as well as
the most frequently sought; but others, such as fathers, former foster carers or
grandparents can be important.

The extent of contact

The amount of contact between members of an adoptive family and a child's
birth family or other previous carers has almost certainly increased in the last
decade or so, although there is little firm evidence of its scale in the past.
However, by the early 1990s half the children in the Lowe and Murch *Support*
study were said by their adopters to have contact with their birth mothers;
22% with their birth fathers; 18% with a maternal grandparent; 11% with a
paternal grandparent; and 17% with other adult relatives. In the case of
siblings, 28% of the children were reported as having contact with one or more
who were in other adoptive homes; 27% with those in care elsewhere; and 18%
with those who were living with the birth family. Overall, 77% of the
respondents said that their child had some form of contact with a birth
relative, and for two-thirds of them the adoption order had already been
granted. However, it should be borne in mind that this part of the study only
covered children who were five or over at placement and that older children
generally have more contact than those who are younger. Furthermore, the
adopters were reporting on any kind of contact. Nonetheless, these figures
probably reflect the shift towards the greater degree of contact that was
accelerated by the philosophy of the Children Act 1989.

The Thoburn research also showed that the amount of contact is likely to
differ as between different groups of children and families and at different
times. For example, children with two black birth parents were more likely to
have had face-to-face contact than those of mixed parentage (45% compared
with 28%), and a few of the young people who had not had contact before did
so after the placement had broken down, whilst others had made contact for
the first time in their mid- to late-teens.

The Thoburn study also provided some data about contact between birth
and adoptive parents, although these were only based upon the small
'intensive' sample. Nevertheless, 35% of the adopters were found never to have
met the birth parents; 28% to have done so only once; 26% on several
occasions after the placement, but only 12% on a regular basis. Of course, no

general conclusions can be drawn from these findings from the early 1980s, but they do remind us that a child's contact with the birth family does not necessarily imply that the adults also have contact. Where this is absent the older child with contact may shoulder a considerable responsibility for the liaison between the two families, an issue which Owen highlights. It should also be noted that in the Lowe and Murch study, 11% of the adoptive parents said that although their child did not have contact with the birth parents they themselves did.

One of the problems in gaining a picture of the nature and extent of children's contact with the birth family is that the types of contact and their frequency are not always specified. Another is that studies do not differentiate consistently between birth mothers, fathers, siblings or other relatives. Different results can be obtained from different combinations. If our understanding of the issues surrounding contact is to be sharpened, much more information is needed about exactly what it comprises.

The Main Points

Contact is a complicated notion and the estimation of its extent varies considerably depending upon how it is defined. There is a need for it to be classified in such a way that, in drawing conclusions, like can be compared with like.

Though common, contact is not universal. Where it occurs it is more likely to be with birth mothers and siblings than with any other relative.

Contact before and after placement

Several of the studies offer evidence that contact is liable to decline once a placement has been made. For example, the Rushton and Dance research on siblings (all of whom were five or more at placement) found that whereas 34% of the children had face-to-face contact with a brother or sister living in the birth family before placement, this fell to 17% thereafter. Although direct contact with siblings who were looked after elsewhere in the care system was much more common, it too declined once the placement had been made: from 78% to 60% by the end of the first year. These were significant differences.

The Quinton and Rushton study, however, did not find a significant reduction in contact in the first year after placement. For example, 36% of the children had 'seen' their birth mother in the year before placement and 32% during the first year after that (although it was unclear whether these were necessarily the same children). The proportion seeing their fathers remained at about 20% throughout.

Despite the limited nature of the evidence about the extent of pre- and post-placement contact it was clear that what had occurred before affected what happened later. For example, those children who were in contact with a birth parent or sibling beforehand were more likely to have retained some contact after the placement than those for whom it had already ceased. In a substantial minority of instances this was because access to their children had been formally terminated with respect to one or both birth parents before the placement. This had happened in around a fifth of the cases in the *Pathways* and in the Malos and Milsom studies, and was probably linked with Quinton and Rushton's finding that the perpetration of abuse was the most common reason for contact having ceased prior to placement.

Both Thoburn and Thomas and Beckford found that post-adoption contact worked well when foster carers who had already set up good arrangements decided to adopt. In such cases birth parents tended not to oppose the adoption.

Where adoption had occurred against the wishes of the birth parents (for example, nearly half of the mothers in the *Pathways* study had had their consent dispensed with by the courts and three-quarters of the applications for freeing orders had been opposed) any subsequent contact was likely to have been difficult to manage. For instance, Lowe and Murch pointed out instances where aggrieved birth parents regarded contact as a route to the eventual resumption of custody; where they used it to make critical comments to the child about the placement and the adopters; and where there had been an attempt to abscond with the child. Other birth relatives who did not approve of the adoption, usually grandparents, could behave in similar ways. Of course, these were the views of the adopters; those of the birth family were not elicited. Even so, it seems plausible that opposition to the very idea of adoption will lead to the manipulation of contact in ways which make it difficult to manage and confusing for the child.

Certain features of the adoption process can also determine the pattern or the terms of subsequent contact. Although contact orders were extremely rare, Lowe and Murch reported that, according to social workers, the courts could encourage contact by requiring them to justify a proposal that there should be none. Furthermore, the promise of contact could be used to persuade reluctant birth parents to give their consent. On the other hand, adopters could feel pressurised to agree to contact for fear that, if they refused, their application would not be supported or that it would be contested.

Thus, there is the possibility that during the prelude to adoption arrangements for contact will be made under duress. When that happens the adopters may become less accommodating once they have the child, or the birth parents may increase their demands for contact. Contact (whatever its precise form) is likely to work best where the adopters are secure in the knowledge that the adoption has been accepted by the birth parents; that is, when they are felt to have given their 'permission' and are not perceived as hostile or antagonistic. The important lesson from this, therefore, is that if it has been decided that contact is in the child's interest it is very important to find adopters who understand the reasons, have been prepared for it and who have the skills and the support necessary to facilitate it.

The Main Points

Decisions taken earlier (sometimes much earlier) in a child's care career are likely to influence the pattern of contacts with the birth family once an adoption placement has been made. That being so, it is of great importance that the possible implications of such decisions for future contact be taken into account at the time.

Contact after placement is likely to be adversely affected (although not necessarily reduced) if adoption has been opposed by the birth family and if they continue to be antagonistic towards it. Skilled social work with such birth families will be required where it is considered to be in a child's interest for unambiguous and beneficial contact to occur.

Planning contact

The studies throw light on several aspects of planning in relation to contact. In the first place, it is plain that the implications of contact of various kinds should be made clear to prospective adopters and linked to their comprehensive preparation and assessment. Similar preparation, as a first step in making feasible plans, should be undertaken with birth parents and children. Likewise, adoption panels should also take account of proposals about contact in their assessment of the overall plans which they are asked to consider. It is not enough simply to say that contact is or is not intended; specific plans for how it is to be accomplished need to be considered from the outset.

None of the studies go into this amount of detail. The Quinton and Rushton study, for example, only examined whether or not social workers had planned for contact – with birth mothers, fathers, or siblings. It had been planned for there to be contact with six of the 55 birth mothers about whom there was information; with the same number from the 34 fathers, and with 10 of the 40 siblings. Plans were unclear with respect to a number of mothers and siblings, but not with regard to fathers. Where the birth parents were concerned matters had usually gone ahead as planned, except that rather more of the children had had contact with their birth mothers than had been foreseen. In the case of the siblings it was the reverse, partly, it was suggested, because families were left to implement these arrangements without assistance and partly because of the reluctance of other carers in the network.

In the Rushton and Dance study plans for face-to-face contact between siblings after placement were formulated for just over a third of the children. There were, however, significantly different intentions depending upon *where* the other siblings were living. It was planned for only 17% of the children to have contact with a sibling who remained with the birth family but for 60% to see brothers or sisters who were living elsewhere in the care system. Nevertheless, in both cases a substantial reduction in contact was planned with siblings in both situations once the placement was made. The explanations offered by social workers for the first of these were that since no contact with the birth parents was now planned, none could be contemplated with the siblings at home with them; that those siblings remaining at home were less likely to be full siblings, and that they had, in any case, been born after the placed child had left. No explanations were forthcoming for why contact with siblings looked after elsewhere was planned to decline except, as already noted, there were sometimes difficulties in 'engaging both sets of carers'.

Other studies considered 'contact agreements' rather than 'contact plans', although there would almost certainly have been an overlap between the two. Agreements (some in writing, some not) were common. Two-fifths of the families who responded to the Lowe and Murch questionnaire, and where there was some form of contact with at least one birth relative, said that they had a written agreement. Others (an unreported proportion) said that they had unwritten agreements which were made and maintained with little or no involvement of the agency. In some cases where the child had been placed, but where an order had not yet been granted, agreements were still being negotiated.

Although the use of written agreements varied between agencies in the Lowe and Murch study, it seemed that whether or not a 'contract' had been drawn up depended upon who was involved. For example, whereas 50% of the families where the child had contact with birth parents had a written contract this fell to 37% for siblings. Most social workers also thought that it was more feasible to have written contracts about the nature of indirect contacts than about arrangements for direct meetings, primarily because there was less likelihood that circumstances would change.

Of course, written contact agreements are not legally binding and cannot be enforced; they depend for their success on the goodwill of the parties involved and this necessitates clear and well-negotiated preparatory work – work that takes into account both the needs of the child and what the adults involved are capable of managing. Thereafter, agreements may need to be reviewed and modified as situations change.

The Main Points

Whether or not contact is to take place is generally planned beforehand. Clear expectations are most likely to be set out with respect to birth fathers and somewhat less often for birth mothers. Plans are least likely to have been formulated in the case of contact with siblings.

In some instances contact failed to occur when it had been intended, whilst in others it happened when it had not. However, there was no indication from the studies of why or when plans did not materialise, or how closely their detailed requirements were observed. Nor was it evident what steps were taken when they were broken. More detailed information is required.

Written agreements were far from universal but they were more common with respect to birth parents (especially where contact was to be indirect) than they were with siblings. In some instances adopters reported that they had unwritten agreements, most of which were managed independently of the agencies.

Direct contact

Rather different issues were reported with respect to the 'management' of direct contact with birth parents than with indirect contact. To start with the attitudes of the adopters were generally more favourable to the latter than to the former. However, as Lowe and Murch concluded, it was not the idea of direct contact that was found to be difficult but the problems thrown up by 'the dynamics of the meetings'. Thoburn's adopters expressed similar sentiments. Altogether, 32% had been unwilling for *any* face-to-face contacts to take place with a parent, but it was pointed out that the kind of information about birth parents that they were given tended to influence their attitudes. However, there was a greater readiness to agree to such contacts with a child's siblings or other relatives. Adopters were generally more hostile to direct contacts with birth fathers than birth mothers.

These attitudes are important since, as both the Thoburn team and Malos and Milsom discovered, continuing contact with birth parents was never imposed against the wishes of the adoptive parents; for example, where future contact was envisaged the court records frequently noted that it would have to be at the discretion of the adopters.

Nonetheless, the Thoburn figures indicate that, even in the early 1980s, there were adopters who were prepared for some degree of face-to-face contact with the birth families. However, this was not to say that such meetings were welcome or that they were without their stresses and strains. The adopters in the Lowe and Murch study explained the reasons. Some spoke of their anxiety at having to admit the birth family into their family, something that could be experienced as a threat to their sense of family identity and parental status. Others were concerned about the destabilising effect that contact could have upon the children. Problems were also reported when, through contact, the birth families continued to regard the child as a full member of their family, an especially difficult situation when they were expected to attend significant occasions such as weddings or funerals. Another practical problem was the issue of presents. Adopters were sometimes at a loss to know whether, and if so how, to regulate the avalanche of gifts that some birth parents showered on their offspring at visits or at other times.

In some cases meetings were arranged at an access centre and, generally speaking, these were welcomed by adopters if they entertained anxieties about the contact. However, their artificial and uncomfortable nature was often described and adopters in several of the studies remarked on the low level of interaction between the children and their birth parents at such meetings. Doubtless had the birth parents' views been obtained these too would have revealed discomfort and uncertainty about such constrained occasions.

In the Lowe and Murch project, some adopters expressed the wish for a social worker to be present at contact meetings in order to check such things as inappropriate behaviour and to reassure and help all concerned. However, there were others who felt that because they often involved supervision these meetings brought social workers into their lives when they and their children were anxious to be free of them. Moreover, as the Quinton and Rushton study found, not all adopters attended contact meetings and some were critical of agencies that insisted that they should. Likewise, as Thoburn and her colleagues pointed out, some birth parents were said not to want to meet the adopters.

The studies identified several problems with respect to direct contact between siblings. First, where siblings lived with members of the birth family there was the problem of controlling the extent of 'secondary' contacts when these were regarded as undesirable. Secondly, where other substitute carers were looking after the siblings it was not always easy to obtain their agreement to meetings, especially if they felt that the placement was insecure. Likewise, some adopters were reluctant for meetings to take place when they considered that they would threaten a rather precarious situation in their family. In this sense, *both* placements probably needed to be fairly secure for both sets of carers to be happy about sibling contacts. Thirdly, not all children wished to see all their siblings. Fourthly, adopters could be concerned about their child having contact with a sibling if that sibling (perhaps because they were in a foster home) had contact with the birth parents which was considered unsuitable. It was hard for them then to explain to their child why they could not have similar contact. Fifthly, adopters were reluctant to support meetings when there had been a history of abuse amongst the siblings, especially sexual abuse. Finally, it should be noted, that because of several of these considerations adopters could be more favourably disposed towards their children meeting some of their brothers and sisters than others.

The Main Points

Although adopters can be sympathetic to the *idea* of direct contact with birth parents, especially for the sake of the children and in order to obtain more information, the practical and emotional realities may weaken their willingness for it to happen.

The 'regulation' of direct contact can be difficult. Many adopters need the support and guidance of a social worker before, during and after such encounters, whether they are personally involved or not. The same is probably true for many of the birth parents and for the children.

Although meetings at contact centres and supervision help to ensure that the agreed limits are adhered to, they are also likely to be uneasy encounters, not least because of their artificiality and the lack of conventions about how they should be conducted.

Planning is clearly necessary if face-to-face contacts with birth parents or siblings are to be successful in fulfilling their purpose. For example, such planning should be linked to the comprehensive assessment and preparation of prospective adopters on all aspects of contact, whether direct or not.

Indirect contact

Most agencies were reported to have had 'letter-box' schemes (95% of them in the Lowe and Murch study) and there also appeared to be a good deal of communication by letter or telephone between the children and their birth families. The frequency and nature of such contacts varied enormously – from a Christmas or birthday card to regular telephone conversations. Children and adults communicated, children communicated with each other and the adults in the respective families did so as well. Whatever the precise nature of these communications they could raise problems. For instance, Lowe and Murch as well as Owen reported that keeping their identity and whereabouts anonymous was a key concern for some families. Many had also experienced difficulty in deciding what to write and how it should be expressed, although hardly any of those who had indirect contact had received help from the agency in doing so. The few examples of sample letters or other guidance were appreciated and these, the authors concluded, should be available more often; but not only to the adopters. Birth parents as well are likely to find difficulty in knowing what to write, either to their children or to the adoptive parents. Written agreements about such matters go only so far; the parties to them may need help in their realisation.

Where communications were routed via the agencies the question of vetting arose. From the information that Lowe and Murch gathered from the agencies it was clear that there was no common policy: some opened and read letters from birth parents before forwarding them to the adopters or to the children, whilst others simply sent them on unopened. None mentioned vetting correspondence travelling in the opposite direction. Sometimes letters were forwarded, sometimes delivered by social workers. The adopters emphasised how important it was for them to know whether or not there had been any vetting, especially of material that might be given directly to the child.

The actual process of vetting raised a number of unresolved issues. Was it a clerical task or was it something that professionals should do? If letters were considered to contain unsuitable material what should be done about it? Should they be returned, censored, destroyed or what? Should there be a follow-up and, if so, of what kind? Lowe and Murch also reported the worries that practitioners expressed about the management of letter-box schemes. Should they be located in local offices or centrally run? What about the sheer volume of the traffic that is building up, especially at Christmas time? If most adoption placements now involve at least some indirect contact, more guidance about all these matters needs to be provided.

Of course, it should not be assumed that all indirect contact involves the agencies as intermediaries. For example, the Romanian study found that a third of the families were exchanging occasional news with the birth parents when the child was six and that for 7% more such contact occurred on a regular basis.

The Main Points

It is important that all those concerned in indirect contact should be clear about its purpose and what it entails; this calls for preparation, negotiation and, in some cases, monitoring.

Help should be available to all involved in framing the content of their communications. Sample letters and guidelines would be welcome.

Careful thought needs to be given to the administration of letter-box schemes. Having developed in a rather piecemeal fashion, they now need to be placed on a more systematic footing, taking into account the resources that that will demand.

Virtually no information was available from the studies about telephone communication. Nor were the possible implications of new communication technologies mentioned; e-mail for instance.

Contacts with foster carers

Contacts with a child's birth family are clearly not the only ones that may need to be made or managed. Certainly, some of the children valued, or would have wished to have had, contact with their former foster carers, especially if they had been with them for a long time. Some telephoned them, others wrote and received letters, whilst yet others made visits from time to time. There were examples of previous foster carers being described by adopters almost as if they were members of their extended family.

However, adopters could also experience problems around such contacts. Some felt that they were in competition with those foster carers who were still regarded with affection by the child. Others worried that the amount of contact was getting out of hand whilst, conversely, there were sometimes concerns that former foster carers were unresponsive to the approaches that they or the children were making. A good deal seemed to turn upon how attached the child and the foster parents had been, upon how well the child's departure from the foster home had been managed, and upon whether careful preparations had been made.

The 'new' adoption is frequently characterised as a three-cornered set of relationships – child, birth parents and adopters; but in some cases it could be four-cornered – with former foster carers included as well. This may add to the complexity of the interactions with which all involved have to deal.

> **The Main Point**
>
> Previous foster carers are important and the question of the extent and nature of a child's continuing contact has to be addressed. Such contacts can be beneficial, but also add a further layer of complexity in the network of relationships.

Contact and outcomes

One of the main questions being asked about contact is its effect upon the child and upon the placement more generally. However, the evidence from these studies remains largely inconclusive.[2] In the Quinton and Rushton research, for example, no significant relationship was found between contact and the levels of children's behaviour problems, nor was there any association between contact with a birth parent and the placement's stability at the end of a year. However, the majority of the new parents said that contact had been either positive or neutral in its effect. Contacts with siblings were generally considered by adopters to be more helpful than those with parents.

Three further points from this study need to be noted. First, various adopters explained that *some* aspects of contact were helpful to the progress of the placement whilst others were a hindrance. Owen reported something similar; namely, that the benefits to the child could be offset by what the parents felt to be disadvantages for themselves or other members of the family. The second point to be borne in mind from the Quinton and Rushton study is that the parents' views about contact were liable to change over time in either direction. A third important observation was that the researchers found the analysis of the impact of contact extremely difficult. The numbers they were dealing with were small and the contacts ranged 'from an hour spent under the supervision

---

2 Although, it has to be said, none of the studies set out specifically to explore this issue. However, for a full review of the overall evidence on the subject see Quinton D, Rushton, A, Dance C and Mayes D (1997), Contact between Children Placed Away from Home and their Birth Parents: Research Issues and Evidence, *Clinical Child Psych and Psychiat*, 2: 393–413; Ryburn M (1998), In Whose Best Interest? – Post-adoption Contact with the Birth Family, *Child and Family Law Quart*, 10: 53–70, and Quinton D and Selwyn J (1998), Contact with Birth Parents in Adoption – a Response to Ryburn, *Child and Family Law Quart*, 10: 349–61.

of a social worker, to an agreement whereby one child periodically stayed overnight with her birth family'.

Thus, the fact that none of the studies showed that contact had a significant effect upon outcome, one way or the other, may have been because the contacts in question were too heterogeneous, because some of their beneficial effects were offset by others that were detrimental and *vice versa*, or because insufficient time had passed for the implications to be detected. Furthermore, the 'outcomes' in question may have been too narrowly defined.

The Main Points

The varieties of contact are so great that it is hard to judge their consequences in *general*. Sense will only be made of the issue when a clearer differentiation of types of contact has been established and the relationship of these to the needs and preferences of individual children determined. It should also be clear what specific benefits the children are expected to gain from the contacts in question.

Even so, outwardly similar contacts are likely to have mixed consequences, partly because of their different impacts on those involved and partly because of the manner in which these can change as time passes.

Although the assessment of these consequences should focus primarily upon the needs of the child, it has to go further and include the possible repercussions for others who are involved since 'contact', by its very nature, entails the interaction of all the participants.

6

Legal and court proceedings[1]

What the children had to say

'Going to court' figured prominently in children's interpretations of the nature of adoption. Memories of both the anxiety beforehand and of the day of the hearing remained vivid. Anxieties revolved around what having to go to court would entail as well as whether or not the order would be granted. Half of the children in the Thomas and Beckford study had had fears about going; others remembered being nervous or worried. One boy (9) explained that he was very scared of the judge because he thought he 'was going to be all mean and hammer the hammer down ...'. There were others too who had had similar images, with people having to take the oath, a jury and the police. One girl (8) at first denied having been to court because she had not been 'bad', although later she admitted that she had gone, but '... not like going for being naughty'. A 14 year-old boy recalled that he had refused to tell his social worker what kind of adoptive family he would like because, if he did, he would have to go to court. Another had said initially that he did not want to be adopted by his foster carers but explained that this was because he knew it would mean appearing in court which, for him, had implied criminality. Reassurances did not always dispel such assumptions. One boy (9) said that although his adoptive mum and dad helped him a lot and said that 'it's all right to go to court' he did not believe them because he thought that he had 'done something wrong'.

The strong association in the minds of many of the children between courts and wrong-doing must be recognised, as must the likelihood that those with disrupted backgrounds will feel blameworthy, even though they are unsure why. Furthermore, a few of the older children would have been to court before as offenders or been witnesses in criminal proceedings. Others would have

1 Only four of the studies (the *Pathways* and *Freeing* reports, Lowe and Murch on *Support* and the Malos and Milsom work) deal with matters that touch upon the legal framework for adoption. They cover both adoption and freeing applications and although these are often discussed alongside each other, and often in a comparative fashion, they are dealt with in separate sections in this report.

been present in care proceedings which may well have been a distressing experience. Indeed, 52% of the children in the *Pathways* research were known to have been involved in previous child-related proceedings and 16% had been the subject of five or more court orders. Not all, of course, would have had to attend court.

Some of the children had absorbed their adopters' anxieties about the hearing: anxieties about the significance of delay, about birth parents changing their minds, about having to face them in court, or about the possibility that the order would be refused. The longer the wait the greater these shared anxieties tended to be. One girl (14) recalled being worried about 'whether it was going to be right and everything'; others were concerned that if they did not convince visiting social workers that they were 'doing well' during the wait the adoption might not go ahead.

In the event, however, most children said that the hearing was less frightening than they had anticipated, although some of the younger ones had found the building large and threatening and the waiting rooms or corridors crowded and disconcerting. The great majority described judges as sympathetic; but some had been uncertain what to say or how to answer questions. There were instances where a solicitor had done all the talking; where the child was seen alone without support; where the judge's robe and wig were remembered as rather frightening, or where he had spoken in such a loud voice that the child was made uneasy. Those who had been given a little present by the judge remembered it with pleasure.

Several children found their court appearance an anticlimax, although parties or other celebrations arranged afterwards helped to make the day a special occasion. The contrast between the short hearing and the long wait had often taken the children by surprise. However, the most commonly recalled reaction was one of relief that the hearing was over and the order made. Children then knew that they were adopted and, as one of them put it, 'nothing else was going to happen. It was just going to be an ordinary life from now on ...'.

The Main Points

Most children are apprehensive about going to court; some will be fearful. It is not only uncertainty about what will happen or about whether the order will be granted that create anxiety, but the association of courts with wrong-doing. Children commonly entertain an image of the court as it might be in criminal proceedings.

Reassurance that all will be well is not always enough to dispel these anxieties. Seeing a video of a typical hearing or making a preliminary visit to the court are likely to be more effective, and adopters might need to be advised as to how best to allay their children's worries.

Although children do not usually find the hearing as frightening as they had expected, courts should still be sensitive to how the experience might be interpreted by those of different ages.

The value of the formal setting and the symbolic nature of the occasion should not be underestimated. The hearing is a significant *rite de passage* and is recognised as such by most children, albeit in their own ways. It should not be unduly hurried.

The length of proceedings in 'agency' adoptions[2]

The *Pathways* report identified several stages in the adoption process. First, for some children who were placed initially on the basis of foster care[3] there was the period between that placement and the panel's approval of it for adoption. The average duration of this interval was 17 months, but there were large variations between the areas in the sample which probably reflected different policies and practices, especially with respect to placements 'with a view to adoption'.

The second stage in the process was that between the panel approval of the placement for adoption and the submission of an application to court.[4] How long this takes depends upon how soon the placement is actually made (if it has not been made already), and upon how quickly the prospective adopters submit an application: some may delay in doing so if they begin to have doubts as difficulties arise. There is also the legal requirement that a child must have lived with the applicants for at least 13 weeks before an order can be made.

The average duration of this second period was a little over five and a half months in the case of 'unfreed' children but two months longer where a freeing order had been made. This could be because these children were older and took longer to settle. Certainly, age was important; for example, in the case of infants under 12 months it took just over three months before an application was lodged with the court but nearly four times as long for those who were

---

2 Here and elsewhere only the domestic 'agency adoptions' are discussed: step-parent adoptions, adoptions by relatives and inter-country adoptions are excluded, except where indicated.

3 The child may have been placed 'with a view to adoption' or the foster carers may have decided to make an application without that having been the original plan.

4 The research does not provide information about the time between *placement* and application.

between five and 10 years old at placement. Furthermore, it was clear that it had taken longer (10 months on average) for an application to have been made where the placement was being contested by the birth parents.

Once an application has been made a schedule 2 report,[5] providing the court with a résumé of all the background information, has to be submitted within six weeks. This marks a third stage in the proceedings. The reports are prepared by adoption agencies or the social services departments to which notice is given of the application to adopt. However, the court records did not enable the *Pathways* researchers to establish how long it had taken for these reports to be submitted or, indeed, what proportion had failed to be completed within the statutory period. However, in their study (albeit some years later and with a sample slanted towards difficult or contested cases) Malos and Milsom found that the average time to elapse between applications and the submission of schedule 2 reports was 13 weeks, well in excess of the six specified in the adoption rules. It took even longer in the case of step-parent applications (a mean of 27 weeks), largely because of the low priority accorded this work.

The interviews with the practitioners in the *Pathways* study threw a good deal of light on why there had been delay in the submission of schedule 2 reports. One reason was the practitioners' lack of experience in undertaking the necessary enquiries and in composing the report. They were not always sure what was needed; for instance, should the report be able to stand as a full record which the child could consult when they were older? Certainly, the small number of cases that some social workers dealt with militated against the accumulation of experience: of those who were interviewed almost half had had to prepare no more than two schedule 2 reports in the previous year, and only a quarter had completed five or more. Such a lack of experience may have accounted for the variable quality of the reports examined in the Malos and Milsom research.

A second reason for delay in submitting schedule 2 reports was said to be the difficulty experienced in locating the information that the legislation specifies. Although two-thirds of the social workers thought that what was on file was sufficient, others found it inadequate and felt obliged to search elsewhere, especially for facts concerning the birth fathers. Furthermore, when they asked for additional information from birth parents they could be met

---

5 These are reports specified in schedule 2 of the Adoption Act, 1976. See Hazell T and Richards J (1998), *Schedule 2 Reports in Adoption: a Guide for Report Writers and their Supervisors*, the Catholic Children's Soc and Univ of Wales Inst.

with an uncooperative response, especially in child abuse cases or where the parents were already opposing the application or considering doing so. How far, some social workers wondered, should they go in their quest for the fuller picture? What was expected of them? Some judges demanded that considerable efforts be made in locating birth parents whilst others were less exacting.

The general pressure under which social services departments found themselves was a third reason offered to account for the delay in completing schedule 2 reports. Where it was only one of many calls upon their time social workers did not give it priority, especially in comparison with protection work where the immediate safety of a child was at issue.

It should be noted that there were cases in both the *Pathways* and the Malos and Milsom studies where the adoption application was not made until the schedule 2 report had been completed and could accompany it: this might have reduced the speed with which the application was submitted after a child had been placed for adoption. Normally, however, the receipt of the schedule 2 report heralded the next and fourth stage; that was the appointment of a reporting officer (in straightforward cases) or a guardian *ad litem* (where a parent is unwilling to agree to the adoption or where there are special circumstances). The *Pathways* study failed to discover from the records how long it had taken for these appointments to be made. However, some of the practitioners who were interviewed (solicitors as well as social workers) complained about delay in this being done, mainly, it seemed, because guardians were in short supply in some areas.

There were, inevitably, further delays whilst the reporting officers or the guardians *ad litem* gathered the material for their reports. In both the *Pathways* and the Malos and Milsom studies this was affected by the complexity of the case, by difficulties in locating the birth parents (especially the fathers), or by parental vacillation. However, both enquiries found that parental opposition lengthened the time taken for the guardians to submit their reports. Indeed, Malos and Milsom discovered that whereas, on average, 11 weeks passed between the schedule 2 reports having been received and the reporting officers finishing their work it took the guardians more than twice as long (24 weeks) to complete theirs, a fact which, they concluded, was largely unavoidable because of all the complexities.

This stage having been completed, the courts could fix the time for a hearing: this might be regarded as the final stage. Repeatedly, the practitioners interviewed in the *Pathways* study complained about the delays caused by the length of time they had to wait for a hearing date, especially in the High Court. However, no data were available about the extent of such delays. The Malos and Milsom research found that, in some cases, a date for the hearing was not set until the reporting officer or the guardian *ad litem* had been appointed. In other instances a date was not fixed until after the reports of these officers had been received. Yet other courts set a date much earlier in the proceedings, risking the need for an adjournment if reports were not available in time.

The *Pathways* study reported that 75% of the adoption applications were resolved at the first hearing; 17% were known to have required more – but mostly two. The court records were unclear in the remaining cases. Contested applications were significantly more likely to go to two or more hearings. This entailed more delay.

Taking into account all the stages between the application and the granting of an adoption order the *Pathways* research found that 12% of the cases had been completed in under three months; 52% within six months, and another 17% between six months and a year. Nine per cent had taken longer than a year, and for 8% the duration could not be determined from the court records. The average time was 6.3 months. Amongst those cases that had been previously freed the average length of time from application to order was significantly less: 3.3 months. Indeed, no application where a child had been freed took more than six months to reach a conclusion.

The Malos and Milsom study obtained a similar overall result. Cases took, on average, 6.2 months from the application to the final hearing, even though the sample over-represented those which were difficult or contested. It should be noted that these 'agency' applications had also been dealt with significantly faster than step-parent applications (which took 9.9 months on average); applications by other relatives (11.3 months), or inter-country adoptions (9.7 months). As in the *Pathways* results Malos and Milsom found that where a child had been freed it had taken much less time from application to order than it had in unfreed uncontested cases. Unfreed but contested cases took much longer.

The Main Points

The average time between the approval of a placement and an adoption application was six months, but the actual duration was determined partly by how much time was devoted to introductory visits; partly by statutory requirements for a minimum length of time for the child to have lived with the prospective adopters, and partly by how swiftly adopters lodged an application with the court. Some hesitate to do so when they are not sure that they want to proceed.

The average time taken by proceedings from application to final hearing was a little over six months, although there were variations by area and large differences as between different types of cases. About 1 in 8 were completed in under three months but nearly 1 in 6 took over a year. The duration was shorter where children had previously been freed but longer where they were older, where the parents had opposed the application and where a guardian *ad litem* had been appointed (the last two circumstances overlapping considerably).

Schedule 2 reports were not often completed within the six-week period specified in the adoption rules. Delay occurred through the inexperience of social workers, the pressure of other work in social services departments, and difficulties in gathering the relevant information.

Reporting officers took nearly as long to submit their reports as the social workers preparing schedule 2 reports. However, problems in actually tracing parents (especially fathers) in order to obtain their agreement figured prominently in the reasons for delay.

Guardians *ad litem* took twice as long to finish their reports as either the social workers involved in schedule 2 work or the reporting officers. However, since they were only appointed in contested or difficult cases a more protracted investigation would be expected, although other factors contributed as well.

There were delays in setting dates for hearings because of crowded court lists but also because of uncertainty about exactly when steps should be taken to find a hearing date. Some courts waited until all the reports were in, whilst others fixed the date earlier. Although this can speed up proceedings it can also lead to adjournments if reports are not ready in time.

Most applications were determined at the first hearing, but those which were not were principally the contested cases. However, contested or not, virtually all (95%) applications were granted; the rest stood adjourned or had been withdrawn.

Thus, delays can occur at various stages and for a variety of reasons, some of which are within the control of the agencies and the courts but some not. Steps could be taken to reduce delays, most notably by according schedule 2 reporting a greater priority and by improving court timetabling; but some delays will be difficult to avoid and may be purposeful and beneficial to the child.

Freeing applications[6]

The principal source of information about freeing applications is Lowe's study which dealt specifically with the matter. His data were drawn from the same samples as the *Pathways* research and comparisons were made between those children for whom freeing procedures had been invoked and those for whom

---

6 The findings reported in this section broadly confirm those of earlier studies on freeing, for example Lambert L, Buist M, Triseliotis J and Hill M (1990), *Freeing Children for Adoption*, BAAF.

they had not. There were pronounced differences. The former were significantly older; more of them suffered from disabilities, especially emotional and behavioural difficulties; significantly more had brothers and sisters as well as coming from larger families[7]; they had been in care on more occasions than those whose adoptions proceeded without the intermediate step of a freeing application; they had experienced more moves since separation from their birth families; a larger proportion had been involved in previous court proceedings of all kinds, and parental access had more often already been terminated.

The practitioners who were interviewed offered a number of reasons for using 'freeing' as well as for avoiding it. In uncontested cases it was considered to be helpful when the mother was willing to give her consent but the child could not be placed at once and, in the case of babies, when 'the mother agrees to adoption but wants to put the issue behind her as soon as possible'. These were the purposes originally foreseen for freeing.

Where there was 'contest' the advantages of a freeing order were considered to be threefold. First, it could reduce prospective adopters' anxiety: the outcome of the placement could be regarded as secure. Furthermore, since it is the agency which takes on the contest with the natural parents in freeing cases the adopters do not usually have to face the ordeal of an appearance in court although they could be called as witnesses. Secondly, once the child is freed the prospective adopters are relieved of certain legal costs and, in any case, some local authorities felt that their own legal departments were better placed to manage the case than the private solicitors who might be engaged by the adopters. Thirdly, some agencies suggested that the children would be less anxious if doubts about what was to happen to them were removed as soon as possible.[8]

The main reason why agencies and staff said that they were disinclined to seek to free a child was because of the delay involved between the application and the granting of an order. Certainly, the evidence showed that it had taken far longer for freeing applications to reach a final hearing than it had for adoption applications.[9] Whereas 79% of the latter had been completed in under nine months only 46% of the former had been dealt with that quickly. Indeed, 30% of the freeing applications had taken between nine and 18 months

---

7 In 38% of the freeing applications there was a parallel application on behalf of a sibling(s).

8 Fifteen per cent of those for whom adoption applications were made in the *Pathways* study had been previously freed.

9 However, it must be remembered that some of these adoption applications would have involved 'freed' children. This would have built in a certain degree of extra speed.

compared with only 5% of the adoption applications. The average time for a freeing application to complete its course was 12.6 months. The causes of these protracted proceedings echoed those listed in the case of direct adoption applications; but the principal reason for the additional delay was that many more of the freeing applications were contested (75% compared with 25%) and, as a result, more of them involved guardians *ad litem*. Another reason for the delay was that a smaller proportion of the freeing than of the adoption applications were settled at the first hearing – only 31% compared with 78%. This appeared to be because far more (22% compared with 4%) of them were actually contested in court and also because (as a result of parental opposition and the complexity of the case) the guardians' reports were not always ready by the date fixed for the first hearing.

The *Freeing* study threw some light upon the question of the timing of placements for adoption in relation to the timing of applications for freeing orders. Twenty-one per cent of the children subject to these applications had already been placed in their adoptive homes and another 35% had been placed during the proceedings. Forty-four per cent were placed after the order had been made. As the authors point out, given the time that it can take to secure a freeing order it is not surprising that some children will be placed before it is obtained, although this runs certain risks for the child and the adopters if the order fails to be granted.

None of the practitioners who were interviewed considered that 'freeing' had been an unqualified success, but none had suggested its abolition. Delay was seen as its most serious shortcoming and suggestions were made for the introduction of mandatory time limits. How far the situation has changed as a result of the considerable growth in the use of freeing applications during the first part of the 1990s we do not know, although there were (and continue to be) considerable variations between authorities.

The Main Points

The children for whom freeing applications were made differed in many respects from those for whom an adoption application was made without recourse to this intermediate step. They had had more chequered care histories, were older and had come from larger families. Their birth parents were more likely to have disputed the agencies' plans than those for whose children a freeing application was considered to have been unnecessary.

In a minority of instances freeing was used for babies whose mothers had agreed to adoption but where, for one reason or another, a placement could not be made immediately. The studies do not indicate the size of this group.

> There were substantial differences between authorities in their readiness to invoke the freeing procedure.
>
> The main advantage of freeing was seen as relieving prospective adopters and children of anxieties about the outcome of a contested application. Its principal disadvantage was the lengthy nature of the proceedings. This was attributed to a number of factors, but mainly to the contest and to its pursuit up to and including the hearing.[10]
>
> A fifth of the children were already placed when the freeing application was made and another third were placed during the proceedings. This runs the risk of upheaval if the order is not made; but virtually all were.
>
> The existence of a freeing order hastens the subsequent adoption proceedings but this, of course, has to be set against the time that it takes to obtain it.

Contest

Both the *Pathways* study and the Malos and Milsom enquiry recognised that it is difficult to define a contested case. However, the criteria that were used were: that an application had been made without the birth parent(s)' agreement; that there had been an application to dispense with that agreement, or that there had been a contested final hearing. Altogether 26% of the adoption applications in the *Pathways* research met one or more of the above criteria for 'contest'. There was much more opposition to freeing applications, 75% of which were contested. However, 'defeat' at this stage will have removed the formal ability of birth parents to resist the subsequent application for adoption.

Contest could be, Malos and Milsom point out, either passive or active. Passive contest is where a parent (usually the mother) refuses to sign the agreement to adoption often 'for fear that the child would think badly of her in future for having "given away" her child'. There was evidence in the records, for instance, that parents sometimes took steps to avoid the agencies or the officers appointed by the courts as a way of not signing. The practitioners in the *Pathways* study echoed these observations, explaining that many found it too painful to sign the agreement or consent form, seeing it as 'signing away' their child. By refusing to sign they could to some extent 'be consoled in knowing that it was the court which made the decision, not them'. However,

---

10 It should be noted that the Adoption Law Review Working Group thought that the advantages were not sufficient to outweigh the disadvantages to the birth family.

having refused to sign the agreement some parents, practitioners reported, did nothing further to oppose the application, even to the extent of not appearing at court for the final 'contested' hearing. There were others who changed their minds. Many of the practitioners recalled instances where the birth mother initially agreed to the application but later had second thoughts. Others moved in the opposite direction. These images capture the anguish that mothers so often feel in having to relinquish their child for adoption.

Malos and Milsom identified three reasons for active contest. First, there were those cases in which the parent(s) objected to the very idea of their child being adopted. Secondly, there were those situations in which there was dispute about arrangements for contact and, thirdly, those where the parents disapproved of the prospective adopters. Of course, there could be a combination of reasons, both passive and active, and these could emerge or subside at different stages of the proceedings.

If parents do not agree to the adoption a 'Statement of Facts' has to be submitted before the parents' consent can be discounted. In the Malos and Milsom study the grounds upon which parental agreement was dispensed with were principally twofold: that a parent was 'withholding their agreement unreasonably' (in 60% of the cases involving the mother and 31% the father), followed by the parent not being able to be found to sign the agreement or being incapable of giving it (11% of the mothers and 27% of the fathers).

Contested cases may mean that one or both of the parties decide to be represented. Delay, the *Pathways* study found, could arise from the inexperience of the solicitors involved. Only 4% of those interviewed said that adoption had accounted for more than a quarter of their work in the previous year (although the small amount of such work available would hardly permit a high degree of specialisation). Furthermore, there were some reports of 'tactical' delays being engineered by those representing prospective adopters, a manoeuvre based upon the assumption that their case would be that much stronger the longer the child had been in placement.

Other delays could occur when the parties were represented and it was necessary to apply for legal aid. Both social workers and solicitors in the *Pathways* study mentioned 'appalling delays'. These were partly attributed to the policy of some local authorities of requiring prospective adopters to apply for legal aid and be refused before they would foot the bill. However, legal aid was not common. According to the Malos and Milsom study in *all* types of adoption applications, 10% of the birth mothers were represented and 45% of the applicants. Of those mothers who *were* represented, 71% had obtained legal aid but only 22% of the applicants. Thus, a very small proportion of all birth mothers had received legal aid, probably because of the strict application of the merits test which gauges the likelihood of a successful action.

Thus, 'contest' not only goes a good way to explain the drawn-out nature of both adoption and freeing procedures but also reflects the mixture of pain, doubt and anger that birth parents feel when confronted with the adoption of their child. Although there is nothing new about such feelings, the resistance to losing a child in this way is, and it represents one of the major changes in the character of adoption that has to be recognised in both policy and practice.

The Main Points

Some contest is essentially passive, parents not wanting to give their consent in a way that could be interpreted as the abandonment or the rejection of their child, even though they might believe it to be in his or her best interests. It might be easier for them if some form of statement or certificate could be permitted which allowed parents to explain their decision, essentially as a record to be held in trust for their child.

A parent's refusal 'to sign' the necessary documents transfers the responsibility for the decision to the court and perhaps lightens their emotional burden.

It is important for social workers to distinguish between passive and active contest; that is, between that which is essentially concerned with negotiation (for example, when it revolves around questions of contact) and that which springs from outright opposition to the very idea. Each has its own implications for practice.

Contest may involve solicitors in representing the parties. This may introduce further delays, as may any application for legal aid.

Differences about who should meet the costs of the representation of applicants need to be ironed out at a policy level, and not case by case.

Tactical delays on the part of solicitors, if they exist, should be discouraged.

Whether contested or not, virtually all adoption and freeing applications are successful. This raises questions about whether the interests of the birth parents are adequately protected.

Some of the legal issues to be considered

None of the studies specifically examined adoption law and that has not been the purpose of this report. However, the *Pathways* report did identify several areas in which the legal framework of the proceedings might be improved.

Avoidable delay

Proceedings were certainly protracted, but it was not easy to decide how much was avoidable. Clearly, some cases are both complicated and contentious and undue haste may be as prejudicial to the child's well-being as undue delay. However, one suggestion was that realistic time limits should be imposed, with the possibility of their being extended when a convincing case for doing so is made. The present six weeks allowed for the completion of schedule 2 reports seems insufficient in the light of the evidence. No time limits apply to any stage of freeing proceedings and none to the listing of cases. The value of time limits is in part that targets are set and in part that undue delays then have to be justified.

Undue elaboration

The number of different reports that are called for might be reduced. BAAF's forms E and F are used for providing information to the panels; schedule 2 reports have to be made in all cases; either a reporting officer's or guardian's report then follows, and if there is an application for dispensing with parental agreement a 'Statement of Facts' also has to be prepared. Most of these reports provide much the same information, the later ones often being an elaboration or summary of those that went before. It seems doubtful whether all these various but similar reports are needed in all instances. Their purposes should be reviewed.

Parental rights

None of the studies interviewed birth parents, but the fact that virtually no contested cases had been won gives cause for concern about whether birth parents are unduly disadvantaged in the present proceedings. Their lack of success in challenging applications in court may have been because they were rarely represented or because the agencies only took 'good risks' to court. If that was so, some of the 'poor risks' may have remained in long-term care. There is also the question of whether, in certain cases, a residence order under the Children Act 1989 might not be preferable to adoption and whether, therefore, judges should be obliged to consider this possibility.

Differentiation of procedures

The emphasis upon 'contest' should not obscure the fact that there are still a good many 'consensual' adoptions. Different proceedings for these cases might be introduced. They might be dealt with for example (with due ceremony) by Registrars of Births. The objection that parents could still withdraw their agreement right up to the last moment might be met by the imposition of a time limit on the period in which this could be done.

7

Support

What the children had to say

The relationships that evolved with their new parents were described by most of the children in warm and positive terms. Many recognised how hard their parents were trying, and had tried, even when there were stresses and strains. They appreciated the help that they had been given and the depth of the commitments that had been made to them. This was true even amongst some of those in the Thoburn study whose placements had disrupted. The children in the Thomas and Beckford project spoke about the comfort and understanding that their parents provided. As one girl (14) explained: 'they are really, really helpful. Because whenever I've got any problems ... I can always talk to [them]'. Others (but not all) welcomed the opportunities that they were given to ask about and discuss their pasts. 'They tell me about adoption and how I got to be here', said one 12 year-old, adding: 'they said why and what really happened'. Another felt that, because he trusted them, he could tell his mum and dad 'a lot of things that's happened in the past'.

Some also acknowledged how their parents had helped them with their education. Others were grateful for kindly discipline ('they tell us what's right and wrong'). Although most of the children in the Thoburn study who had been placed trans-racially also spoke in a positive fashion about their white adopters, both they and those placed with black parents considered that black families had the advantage over white families in helping them to deal with questions of identity and problems of racism.

There was little evidence from what the children said to suggest especially strained relations with adoptive siblings or other children in the household, including brothers and sisters. However, where adoptive siblings were spoken of warmly and were regarded as supportive they were mostly older adolescents or young adults, and considerably older than the adopted child. Adoptive grandparents were important for some of the children, as were certain family friends. Half the children in the Thomas and Beckford study said that their pets were important sources of comfort. Thus, although the children considered that their adoptive parents (sometimes one more than the other) provided them with their primary support, there were other sources as well. However, social workers were mentioned in only a few cases although these contacts had often ceased by the time of the interviews.

Relationships at school were a prominent issue for many children. Their peers were at least curious about their adoption and sometimes this curiosity was persistent and hostile. A third of the children in the Thomas and Beckford research said that they had been bullied, although they did not necessarily attribute this to their adoptive status, more often saying that it was because they were 'different'. This may have had something to do with difficulties in forming peer relationships. Whatever the explanation there was a need for support. Some found it in close friends and in belonging to a gang – achieving safety in numbers. Some gained special support from certain teachers who were referred to with affection. Knowing and confiding in other adopted children was also supportive and, in this respect, some mentioned the value of the camps or parties that certain agencies organised for them.

One of the things that was important for most children at school was the ability to retain control of information about themselves. They found it disquieting not to know who knew what and therefore who might be saying what about them. The wish to control personal information was related to the problem of explaining why they had been adopted, particularly when there was a background of abuse. Black children placed with white families (or those whose adoptive parents were obviously older than those of their classmates) could not, of course, avoid having to offer or imply an explanation. Help in resolving the dilemma of 'what to say' was welcomed.

The Main Points

Adopted children obtain support mainly from their adoptive parents, even when relationships may be strained. Nevertheless, other sources of support are also important to them and should not be ignored.

Support at school is often needed, particularly the support of teachers and other children – through friendships and group membership. Schools need to take account of the needs of vulnerable children in their policies and procedures.

As well as emotional support adopted children are likely to need practical help; for example, in explaining their circumstances to others and, in some cases, in dealing with the behaviour of others towards them – whether this be bullying, scapegoating or racism.

The challenge of new relationships

It is clear from what both the children and the adopters said that adjustments to new relationships and to new situations are difficult to make, especially during 'the period of transition'.[1] During this time children have to deal with the loss or recasting of previous attachments whilst, at the same time, they have to adapt to a new family and often to a new school and to a new circle of peers. Over and above this, most of the children will have gone through a series of disruptions in their relationships already, many of which will have had a damaging effect. In the Quinton and Rushton sample, for example, two-thirds of the children had experienced four or more admissions to care, and over two-thirds had had four or more placements. The other studies painted a similar picture, emphasising the extraordinary challenge that yet another placement was likely to pose. Obviously, supporting a child through such a demanding transition has to start with sensitive and well-timed preparation, but that will not necessarily ensure the smooth formation of new attachments.[2] The re-attachment process, as Quinton and Rushton emphasise, may be slow or fail to develop altogether. By the end of a year, however, as we have seen, 43% of the children in their study were considered to have made 'good' (mutual) attachments; 30% were showing signs of attachment 'developing', but for 27% there were serious difficulties of relationship with both parents. Where these difficulties existed there were also likely to be difficulties with other children. Both the children and adults in these problematic circumstances will need skilled and continuing support.

Of course, formal services are not the only source of support: family and friends are also important. However, some people pointed out that once they had embarked upon adoption their existing informal support began to diminish, particularly if there were those who disapproved of what they were doing or who found the child's behaviour unacceptable. Children too are likely to be confronted with the need to establish new sources of informal support. Both they and their adopters, therefore, may need extra formal support whilst new patterns of informal support are being established.

---

1 It should be noted, of course, that the follow-up periods in most of the studies were relatively short and that the whole of the 'research period' could well be regarded as covering a transitional phase.

2 For a fuller discussion of these issues and a basis for classification see Howe D (1998), *Patterns of Adoption*, Blackwell.

As well as the need for the adopters and the placed child to be supported there are also the children who are already established in the household to be considered. Not only will they have to come to terms with the newcomer (who may be viewed as a usurper) but also with the modification of family relationships. Yet Quinton and Rushton found that 40% of the established families in their study did not think that the needs of their birth children had been sufficiently taken into account by social workers. It is important for the 'chains' of support to be appreciated. In this case the parents themselves may need support in supporting their birth children and that support, in its turn, may manifest itself in an easier transition for the placed child.

> ### The Main Points
>
> Many children placed for adoption will have experienced numerous prior disruptions which may have damaged their self-esteem or confidence and made them wary of placing too much reliance upon new attachments. For such children the multiple nature of the readjustments which they are called upon to face are daunting. They will need support.
> Social workers, teachers or other professionals can provide some of the support that children need. However, most day-to-day support will have to be given by the new parents. They should be able to do this better if they, in their turn, are well-supported.
> Informal networks are important in the provision of support, but they may change as a result of the placement. Social workers should be aware of the significance of this both for the adopters and the child, and consider ways in which informal support outside the family might be strengthened.

Emotional and behavioural problems

A child's emotional or behavioural problems present a second area of difficulty which is likely to call for support as a placement proceeds.[3] Quinton and Rushton assembled information about children's troubling behaviour from what they were told by the parents. In their 'free accounts' only three sets of parents (5%) said that they had faced no particular challenges in the first month with respect to their child's behaviour. The other 58 described a total of 140 difficulties, the majority of which (71%) were rated as both serious and

---

3 This said, however, it should be recognised that the behaviour of others – classmates at school, other children in the household or the adopters themselves – may pose problems for the placed child.

frequent. Most involved problems of conduct such as defiance, disobedience, displays of temper or abusiveness. Far fewer concerned children's emotional distress; for example, anxiety, worrying and fears of various kinds.

The parents were asked for their views again 12 months after the placement. Some problems had been resolved whilst others had worsened. Of the 61 children in the sample two were described as problem-free throughout the year and for eight of them all the difficulties were considered to have been overcome. At least one of the original problems was resolved for 21 children whilst 27 retained all of them to some degree. Serious new problems arose during the course of the year for two-thirds of the sample, often in addition to the existing problems.

Sexualised behaviour (for instance, masturbation in public, sexually precocious language or sexual behaviour towards other children or the parents themselves) gave rise to much worry. There were 12 such cases during the year (20%) although in only eight of them was past sexual abuse known or suspected. On the other hand, 14 children who were known to have been sexually abused did *not* show signs of sexualised behaviour, a finding that warns against too ready an assumption that sexual abuse before placement necessarily leads to sexualised behaviour in other contexts.

In order to obtain comparable information for all the children Quinton and Rushton next guided parents through a list of emotional and behavioural difficulties and asked them to say which of them they had had to face. This produced a rather different picture from that derived from the parents' unguided accounts. Considerable distress, anxiety and worrying amongst the children, as well as inattentive and restless behaviour were found, but fewer conduct disorders.

The researchers also applied two of the standard psychiatric classifications of difficulties (the DSM-IV of the American Psychiatric Association and the Rutter A2 Scale) to these results in order to assess the degree to which they reached a level that satisfied clinical definitions of disturbed emotional and behavioural development in children. Both scales indicated that around 55% of the children had clinically significant problems.[4] Emotional disorders; anxiety, fears, school refusal, sleeping problems, chronic unhappiness, depression, poor attention and over-activity, were the most common conditions. The overall picture was much the same after 12 months as it had been one month into the placement.

---

4 The authors emphasised that it should not be assumed that the 45% of children who did not meet the criteria for clinical disorder were necessarily free of symptoms: the average number of their problems was still substantial.

The Rutter A2 Scale has been used in relation to the general child population where a rate of disorder of 12% was found. It has also been applied to children in care amongst whom the rate varied between 25% and 30%.[5] Clearly, the rate of 55% in the Quinton and Rushton study was significantly greater. However, the children involved were all five or over. The Romanian study was the only one dealing exclusively with children placed under five. At four years of age 6% of them were assessed as exhibiting autistic or semi-autistic behaviour and 3% showed marked and 11% moderate symptoms of attachment disorder, principally in the form of disinhibition. However, more had displayed such behaviour earlier, suggesting that recovery was possible with sensitive caregivers; but follow-up at six also indicated a good deal of persistence.

These detailed results show that many of the new parents were having to care for some very disturbed children. Indeed, given the scale of disturbance amongst the children it might have been expected that special help, by way of treatment and advice, would have been provided by the mental health services. In fact, as emerged from the Lowe and Murch and from the Owen studies, such help was thin on the ground and when it was provided it was often concentrated upon children who had been sexually abused. Certainly, the parents in the Quinton and Rushton study most frequently expressed the need for support with respect to problems of managing and controlling disruptive behaviour. They did not see as much need for help in dealing with the emotional problems which afflicted many of the children. In the understandable desire to respond to what most troubles adopters these problems may be overlooked.

The Main Points

Challenging and difficult behaviour is liable to occur amongst children placed for adoption from care and to cause the new parents considerable stress. Sexualised behaviour gives cause for special concern and this would indicate that where such behaviour was known to have occurred before, children should receive appropriate counselling or therapy and rather special preparation.

The rate of clinical disorder amongst the children in the Quinton and Rushton study was almost five times greater than that found in the general child population and around twice that which has been discovered amongst groups

---

5 See Rutter M, Tizard J and Whitmore K (1970), *Education, Health and Behaviour*, Longman; and Rowe J, Cain H, Hundlebury M and Keane A (1984), *Long-term Foster Care*, Batsford.

of children 'looked-after'. Such results indicate the severity of the problems that adoptive parents may encounter, a level of severity that warrants skilled and specialised support and treatment, especially from the mental health services; and not least for children's emotional problems that do not always prompt parents to seek help.

Relationships outside the family

The question of managing defiant or aggressive behaviour may have been so prominent in the minds of adopters because its repercussions went beyond the home. It could raise problems for them with the schools, with neighbours, with relatives and with friends. In that sense it was liable to have public consequences that caused the parents additional anxiety and frustration.

There are other aspects of relationships outside the immediate family that also have to be taken into account; for instance, those between the adoptive and birth families. The norms and conventions that apply to these interactions are by no means clear. Nearly a third of the new parents in the Quinton and Rushton study, for example, said that they needed help in negotiations with the birth parents. Likewise, in the Lowe and Murch study many families indicated that they welcomed guidance about how best to deal with such relationships.

Another major area in which 'outside' relationships may pose a problem is school. The Quinton and Rushton team asked teachers to complete the Rutter B Scale (dealing with children's behaviour at school). For purposes of comparison a control group was also drawn from classmates. At one month the placed children showed considerably more problems than their peers and more than the general population of school children. Fifty per cent of the boys scored above the threshold point for disorder and 29 per cent of the girls.[6] Restlessness and poor concentration were the most common problems. In addition, the teachers' ratings, as well as what the parents reported, showed that there were substantial problems in the children's relationships with other children; in particular, because of an inability to pay attention when playing games; a poor level of understanding of the rules; over-enthusiasm in interactions; insensitivity to the feelings of other children; quarrelling, and aggressive behaviour. There was little change over the year.

---

6 The scales were completed more often for the boys than for the girls, so this comparison should be treated with caution.

The Romanian study also assessed children's behaviour at school. Hyperactivity and inattention were common and increased considerably between the ages of four and six. The nature and extent of pretend play was also investigated: whether it was solitary or interactive, whether there was shared enjoyment, how far the wishes and feelings of others were taken into account, and the importance that language assumed. The results were compared with a control group. As early as four years of age the Romanian group had more problems in their play activities. This suggests that signs of difficulties in these relations may well be apparent in the pre-school years, relations which should be capable of being observed and reported even by staff not trained specifically for such work.

There are, of course, issues about the support that the children may need with their education, but these results make it clear that both they and their adoptive parents may also need support in dealing with problems of relationships at school. However, the social workers in both the Lowe and Murch and in the Quinton and Rushton studies did not seem to have provided such support, although only a handful of the parents commented on it adversely largely, it seemed, because they (like the social workers) saw negotiations with the school as being their responsibility; but they might nevertheless have welcomed professional support. How far they had received it from teachers or educational psychologists was not reported, but three-quarters of the parents in the Lowe and Murch study said that they had found the schools 'helpful' and Owen also described favourable reports about the contacts that the parents in her study had had with the schools. However, it should be borne in mind that a number of the children in her sample attended special schools which may be better attuned to providing support to both children and their parents than mainstream schools.

The Main Points

The relationships between the adoptive family and the birth family are liable to be complicated, unfamiliar and stressful. Support is likely to be needed for all concerned. Social workers may have a role to play in its provision.

The relationships of the children at school are likely to be difficult and to have consequences that also create stress for the parents. However, there was little social work involvement in school matters, although assistance may have been forthcoming from teachers. Both the adoptive parents and the social workers assumed that it was the former who were responsible for sorting out issues connected with the school; but additional help should be offered, perhaps by educational advisors.

Practical and financial matters

Only the Owen and the Lowe and Murch studies reported in detail on the practical needs of the families and on the support that was provided in the form of domestic help; child care assistance; the adjustment of employment, and financial aid.

Although several of the single adopters in Owen's sample expressed the wish for more help around the house, there were no reports of local authorities providing or paying for it, although some of the children would certainly have been considered to have been severely disabled. Similarly, Lowe and Murch found only one instance amongst the 226 families in their cohort where a local authority had provided domestic help, although others may have purchased it privately.

At the time of her interviews, two-thirds of the parents in the Owen study were in paid employment (nearly half full-time) and hence were having to devise ways of combining this with child care, although many had applied for a child of school or nursery school age so that they could continue working. The problems of combining work and child care were often resolved by these single adopters by virtue of the nature of their work, or because they modified it after the placement. Those who continued in their employment without making changes were mainly professional and business people who enjoyed a good deal of autonomy at work as well as the support of colleagues and employers. Others changed their employment in order to accommodate the care of their children. A number moved to working at home, and childminding was one way in which this was engineered. Only two gave up work in the first six months of the placement, although a few others did so later when further adoptions and the accompanying allowances made it necessary and possible to do so.

Thus, although this information about the way in which single adopters accommodated the demands of employment and child care is limited it serves to make the point that arrangements for child care need to be supported. Indeed, given some of the difficulties that all adopters are likely to face, the issue goes well beyond single adopters alone in terms, for example, of the flexibility or rigidity of employment practices and the availability of various other practical supports such as respite care. In their postal survey Lowe and Murch found that about a fifth of the families had been provided with such relief at some time, but another 30% said that they did not know of its availability, although virtually all the agencies said that it could be available. Some of those who knew of the possibility did not apply, fearing that the standard of care might be inadequate, or because they were apprehensive about the consequences when they resumed the child's care.

Adoption allowances and other financial assistance are another important practical support. Amongst the families in the Lowe and Murch postal survey 61% said that they had received an adoption allowance.[7] However, there was little consistency in policies about payment, and one of the principal criticisms was that information and advice about such allowances (and indeed about other allowances) was not provided until it was requested, despite the fact that virtually all the agencies in the study said that they offered *some* cash allowances.

The list of issues surrounding the payment of adoption allowances (as recounted by the adopters in the Lowe and Murch study) was both long and varied.[8] It included: the widely different amounts of the allowances; the uncertainty about how long payments would continue and at what level (an important matter for those increasing their mortgage in order to provide more space); confusion about the treatment of the allowance for taxation purposes; not being able to apply for an allowance retrospectively (for instance, upon redundancy); a lack of clarity about the nature of the means-testing; the failure to settle the question of allowances before the placement; variations in the starting points for payment (either at the placement or not until the order was made); and the curtailment of allowances at 18 (an important matter if the children were severely disabled or proceeding to higher education).

Adoption allowances carry, therefore, the hallmarks of a discretionary system that suffers from uncertainty and variation and which conveys the impression of a charitable donation to which the applicant has no automatic right. Not infrequently adopters reported that the social worker had had to 'fight for them' to receive payments from their authorities.

The adoption allowances regulations require authorities to review payments each year, a rule that, according to both the Owen and the Lowe and Murch evidence, was often ignored. Indeed, almost two-fifths of the agencies in the latter study admitted that they did not undertake annual reviews. Some did so every two years, others when they could. The adopters tended to be unclear

---

7 Only 4% of the families in the full cohort of the Thoburn study were known to have received an adoption allowance, but many of these placements would have been made before the scheme was fully operational; 73% of the *children* in Owen's study attracted an allowance.

8 These findings generally confirm previous studies; for example, Hill M, Lambert L and Triseliotis J (1989), *Achieving Adoption with Love and Money*, National Children's Bureau.

about reviews. Some welcomed their absence or infrequency, particularly if they thought that this deferred a reduction or withdrawal of the allowance. Others had the impression that it was only when this was likely that the authorities held a review. Conversely, some of the adopters in the Owen study believed that the uprating of their allowance had been delayed for want of a review.

Adoption allowances are not the only way in which adopters can receive financial help. The families in the Lowe and Murch postal enquiry had received variously: assistance in meeting the cost of legal representation; initial grants for such things as furniture and school uniforms; help with the travel costs associated with contact or hospital visits; payments for private therapy, counselling, and for special lessons. However, these were all one-off payments that had usually to be asked for and granted (or not) at the discretion of the authority. It seemed more common for respondents to complain that they had been denied them than to say that they had been provided.

The importance of allowances and payments should not be underestimated. Virtually all the respondents in Owen's study said that the extra financial costs associated with the adoption had been more than they had expected. Other respondents said the same. For example, 30% of those interviewed in Thoburn's enquiry reported that they were 'sometimes or often' short of cash. Others complained that, as adopters, they were unable to use a local authority's 'supported lodging' scheme when children reached later adolescence and when such a move could prevent a total breakdown of relationships. They had to arrange to pay for such a solution themselves, unlike foster carers. Likewise, if a boarding school seemed to be the answer to their children's problems they had to pay for that too.

Thus, some of the confusion and discontent surrounding adoption allowances and other forms of financial assistance sprang from comparisons with what was available to foster carers. Some adopters had fostered the children before adopting them; others had fostered other children, and some authorities had paid a fostering allowance during the placement until the adoption order had been granted. Some of those who had earlier received a foster care allowance for the child were denied an adoption allowance. Those who were more fortunate nevertheless often compared the level of the allowance for adoption unfavourably with what they had received as foster carers. Furthermore, they were now means-tested and there was no longer a contractual basis for the payments. Some pointed out that this hardly encouraged foster carers to adopt.

> ### The Main Points
>
> Practical and financial needs should not be underestimated, especially as more
> adopted children are now older, may suffer certain disabilities or have other
> needs that entail special expenditures. Domestic help, child care or respite
> care may be needed, especially where parents are in employment, but, apart
> from some respite care, there was little evidence of it having been provided.
> Financial help, whether by way of adoption allowances or one-off payments, was
> inconsistent: in some cases it was generously and readily provided whilst in
> others it was difficult to obtain and reluctantly offered. Many adopters did not
> know what they might reasonably expect, when and on what conditions.
> There is a strong case for these matters to be made clear at the outset but,
> over and above this, for financial help to adopters to be put on a less
> discretionary footing. There is also a case to be made for the harmonisation of
> foster care and adoption allowances.

Support by whom?

Professional support

Social workers provided most of whatever professional support had been
offered to the children and the families.[9] At the start of the placement this was
shared between the child's social worker (CSW) and the family social worker
(FSW) although, as Lowe and Murch found, in those adoptions arranged by a
voluntary agency the FSW played a more significant role than in those
approved by a local authority. Even so, there was a common perception on the
part of adopters that the CSW's role was to assist the child and that the FSW
was to support them. This seemed to reflect the assumptions that were made
by the social workers themselves. Even so, the adopters could be uncertain, as
Thoburn found, about who should be approached for what, especially when
what was needed was not clearly connected with the child or with them.
Furthermore, even if the adults are clear about the roles of the two social
workers it does not follow that the children are, especially if they have
encountered other social workers (or, indeed, the same social worker) in
different roles.

As time passed so the pattern of social work support changed: visits
became less frequent and the CSWs played a lesser part. Nonetheless, Quinton

---

9 The Romanian adoptions were the significant exception. Only 4% were receiving
  support from social workers at the time of the first interviews.

and Rushton found that, even after a year, support from the CSW was continuing for 63% of the families and that offered by the FSW for 74%. All social work support had ceased for 15% of the cases; but in these instances an order had been made *and* stability was judged to have been achieved. Both the CSW and the FSW were still involved with half of the families 12 months after the placements had been made, although it should be remembered that in some of these cases the adoption order still remained to be granted and some of the placements were with foster carers. Where visiting was continuing it occurred, on average, every five or six weeks for CSWs and FSWs alike. In the Thoburn cohort 70% of those for whom information was available had been visited at least every two weeks for the first three months, but with a falling off thereafter. The picture was very different for the Romanian adopters, some of whom pointed out that the welfare *supervision* which applies to all non-agency placements implies monitoring rather than support. The issue arises, therefore, as to who should provide *support* in those cases where the agency does not have statutory responsibility for the child prior to the application to adopt.

Thus, the Romanian placements apart, there was a good deal of 'support' during the early stages of the placement. However, those studies which included placements that had been in existence for several years (Thoburn's and Owen's in particular) showed that social workers were likely to disappear from the scene as time passed. Indeed, there were clearly some adopters and children who had been anxious to distance themselves from the agencies, feeling that their position would not be 'normalised' whilst they remained involved with social workers.

Nevertheless, even when routine visiting had ceased, the help of social workers could be sought at times of crisis or about special issues. About half of the adopters in the Lowe and Murch postal survey said that they had needed assistance with what they described as an emergency. Most had been able to find the help that they sought (not necessarily, of course, from the agencies); but a fifth said that they had not. It was plain from several of the studies that there were specific times during the placements when adopters or children felt in need of *immediate* support. Such circumstances demanded help to be 'on call', to be provided quickly by staff who were competent and who were familiar with the particular background. Both adopters and children should know to whom they can turn when they feel that there is an urgent need for help. Lowe and Murch asked the agencies in their survey what provision they made for such emergencies. Almost all said that they had arrangements in place, but typically through emergency duty officers or teams or the availability of a telephone number which, especially in the case of the voluntary agencies, could be the social worker's home number.

Whether there was a crisis or not, the Quinton and Rushton study concluded that 'parents seem to have to rely almost entirely upon the strengths and weaknesses of the social work service' for professional support. Indeed, only 20% of them said that they had been helped by any other professional during the year. However, Lowe and Murch reported that 38% of the adopters in their postal survey had had contact with their GP in connection with the adoption and, in most cases, that they had found it helpful. The rate of 'helpful support' from GPs was much greater in the Romanian study (91% of the adopters noting it), and this was the only enquiry in which the support of health visitors was mentioned (by 84% of the adopters). This probably reflected the fact that the children were much younger than those in the other studies. However, given that health visitors *are* often involved with the families of older children who are disabled it is surprising that it was only in the Romanian study that they made a supportive appearance. Of course, some professionals, such as solicitors, are usually only involved at particular stages of the adoption so that questions about who has been helpful may be answered differently at different times.

Children with learning difficulties or physical disabilities were excluded from both the Rushton and Dance and the Quinton and Rushton studies. By contrast, they were numerous in Owen's sample and she reported that their adoptive parents had often received good support from educational and medical services. This suggests that the existence of these conditions enabled parents to draw on such other services in a way that was not so readily open to adopters of more 'ordinary' children.

The Main Points

At least in terms of the frequency and duration of visiting, the social work services had provided considerable support to most of the adoptive families. Usually, it had continued over the period of the 'transition'. Thereafter, there was a gradual reduction.

Adopters were more likely to turn to the FSW for support rather than to the CSW. Even so, more clarification about who could be expected to do what would be helpful.

Much of the social work support was focused upon the adopters rather than upon the adoptive family as a whole.

Emergencies or crises occur and call for the rapid provision of support. A swift and well-informed response should be readily available.

Little support was obtained from professions other than social work, although the adopters of the Romanian children (who were much younger) had more contact with doctors and health visitors.

Informal support

The Thomas and Beckford study showed that children turned first and foremost to their adoptive parents for support and, as Quinton and Rushton found, couples usually turned to each other. In the Lowe and Murch study, adopters said that those who had helped them most (apart from their partners) had been friends (93%), followed by relatives (89%). Although only 35% had had contact with other adopters, almost all who had had found them helpful. It should also be noted that those who were involved in church organisations (28%) considered them to have been supportive. The support of friends and relatives did not figure as prominently in the replies of the adopters in the Quinton and Rushton study. At 12 months only a third said that they had found support amongst their relatives (apart, that is, from their spouses). Rather more (just over a half) had mentioned their friends. The differences between these two findings may be attributable to differences in the interpretation of 'helpful contribution' and 'support' and to the time in the adoption process when the replies were given. There were also some adopters who drew back from discussing their problems with relatives or friends in order to protect the child and themselves from adverse or critical reactions.

Single adopters do not have a partner to whom they can turn for support but, with only a few exceptions, Owen found that those in her study were well supported by their network of relatives and friends. One in 10 had a parent living with them, and the single adoptive mothers tended to have particularly strong bonds with their own mothers and with their sisters, aunts and grandmothers, although contact with the males in the family were not ignored, especially if the adopted children were boys.

It is equally important to appreciate what support, if any, children receive from the brothers and sisters with whom they are placed or, indeed, from other children in the household. The Rushton and Dance study provides some insights, albeit chiefly about brothers and sisters. During the early months siblings were reported as showing mainly positive feelings towards each other; but for about a fifth no such feeling was discernible. By the time of the interviews at 12 months the overall situation had improved, although there had been movements in both directions. However, the researchers also interviewed a control group of siblings living with their birth parents with which they were able to compare their results. At three months there was no difference between the study and the control groups in the extent to which they engaged in joint activities, but both rivalry and conflict were significantly more frequent and more serious amongst the siblings who had joined new families. Furthermore, whereas the control group's disputes were mainly verbal those amongst the placed siblings much more often involved serious fighting. The pattern was similar after 12 months.

These results sound a note of caution against a too ready assumption that the relationships between siblings placed together will necessarily be harmonious and mutually supportive, and point to the need, in some cases, for sibling relations to be assessed well before placement. However, the rationale for placing siblings together probably lies elsewhere, particularly in its lifelong value both in providing continuity and in the affirmation of identity. Adopters may need to be helped to appreciate these advantages both during preparation and later.

The informal support of adoptive families can come from more organised sources than family and friends; for example, from mutual support groups such as Parent to Parent Information on Adoption Services (PPIAS; now renamed Adoption UK); or from membership of organisations of parents with children suffering from certain conditions or disabilities. However, although membership of such groups was not widespread amongst those in Owen's study, 30% of the adopters in the Lowe and Murch postal survey had contact with an adoption support group and 28% with PPIAS. Sometimes social workers had arranged a link family. The adopters in the Romanian study in particular had formed strong supportive networks. Eighty-two per cent of the families had contact with other families who had adopted from Romania and the Adopted Romanian Children Society was formed in 1990. The support of others with similar experiences was said by adopters in several of the studies to be more helpful and more acceptable than a professional service. Those who provided this support gained satisfaction and confidence from doing so. Indeed, it was not uncommon for the adopters in both Thoburn's and Owen's studies to explain that they did not regard themselves primarily as *consumers* of support but rather as *providers* to the children and to others.

The Main Points

Family and friends can be important sources of support. Their attitudes and likely availability should be routinely taken into account in assessing a family's resources.

Adopters find the support of others with similar experience both valuable and acceptable, although comparatively few in these studies belonged to organised support groups or had been paired with a 'link family'. The adopters of children from Romania were the exception.

Not all children will necessarily find support in the brothers and sisters with whom they are placed. Indeed, the whole question of the extent to which placed children are supported or not by other children is clearly important. If the availability and effect of informal support is as important as the studies indicate, so too may be the undermining influences; for example, in the sense of community isolation or hostility.

Evaluating support

The recipients' evaluation of social work support

The adopters' assessments of the social work support that they had received were generally positive, although there were notable exceptions. Eighty-nine per cent of the respondents in the Lowe and Murch postal survey had found the FSW 'helpful' and 75% the CSW. Likewise, 80% of those interviewed by the Thoburn team expressed broad satisfaction with the level and content of the social work provided. However, the proportion in the Quinton and Rushton study who were satisfied was lower: 42% of the parents described both their CSW and FSW as supportive; about the same proportion had felt supported by only one of them, whilst 15% said that they had not been adequately supported by either. The rate of satisfaction was substantially lower (40%) amongst the adopters of Romanian children, possibly because the social workers were interpreting their role in terms of assessment and supervision rather than support.

However, the levels of satisfaction varied depending upon precisely which need was being considered. In the Quinton and Rushton study there was widespread satisfaction (90%) amongst those who sought reassurance, whether it was provided by the CSW or the FSW. Those who looked for help in managing difficult behaviour, completing administrative tasks, or obtaining more information about the child were less satisfied (a third had found the help that they had been offered on these matters unsatisfactory). Least satisfaction was expressed about support in meeting material needs (only 40% being content).

Thoburn also pointed out that 'those who were not satisfied tended to be critical about a particular part of the service at a difficult period'. Likewise, although the general level of satisfaction was lower amongst the adopters in the Romanian study it was the 'unhelpfulness' of social services departments in responding to their application for a home study (a third had had to apply at least twice) which appeared to have been responsible for their dissatisfaction in the first place, although they also felt that the local authorities had been unsympathetic and discouraging to overseas adoptions. Thus, not only were different areas of support valued differently by adopters but quite specific shortcomings could jeopardise relations to such an extent that the whole of the social work service came to be regarded in an unfavourable light. Conversely, as Thoburn found, positive links made at the time of the home study could be carried forward into later stages of the placement, especially if the social worker involved remained unchanged.

Of course, criticism could be reserved for a particular worker, and the presence of a CSW and an FSW performing somewhat different functions could provide the opportunity for invidious comparisons as well as choice. Indeed, adoptive parents were more likely to view the FSW as an ally and collaborator than the CSW. In contrast, the CSW was seen as having loyalties that were divided between the adoptive family and the birth family, and between the adopters and the child. Several of those interviewed in the Thoburn study felt that the CSWs were not 'even-handed' in their approach, tending 'to take the child's side' (as, indeed, their role demanded), which made the adopters feel blamed for anything that seemed to be going wrong.

The features of a social workers' support that adopters valued most were consistently reported in the studies. Broadly speaking they were: its ready availability; a warm and trustworthy relationship; reliability (especially in doing what was promised when it was promised); the opportunity for unhurried discussion (not least the opportunity to share 'the good things'); informed guidance and advice about day-to-day problems and, as we have seen, the sense of committed allegiance. When these were absent dissatisfaction mounted, although it seemed to be particularly evident when social workers were considered not to possess sufficient skill or experience to advise about 'what to do'; when they were unreliable; unnecessarily intrusive, or 'obstructive'. Furthermore, what parents wanted and what social workers thought was needed could be at odds and this could account for the dissatisfaction that some of the adopters felt with what was offered.

The 'demand' for support

One important determinant of what social work support is provided is the difficulty that a case presents. Another is the 'demandingness' of the family. Owen noted that one of the differences between the single adopters was their attitudes to social work help. Those who were new to parenting and who mainly had younger and less problematic children placed with them looked to their social workers for advice about such matters as feeding and sleeping routines. Many were pleasantly surprised that the kinds of problems which they had been led to expect did not materialise or not in as severe a form as they had anticipated.

By contrast, those who were experienced did not readily seek social work help. They had no strong inclination to fulfil unrealistic parental ambitions, were tolerant and usually unruffled. However, most had adopted some time ago and had been out of touch with the agencies for several years. For many, their support came primarily from their family and their community. However, Owen noted that their children – particularly the older adolescents – might have benefited from more social work support, an observation that draws attention to the possible dangers of interpreting the demand for social work support only through the requests of the adopters.

Those amongst Owen's adopters who worked in a professional capacity in services for children set themselves high standards. They took pride in their skills and had invested a good deal of their professional self-esteem in the success of the placement. Even so, they generally worked well with the social workers, enlisting their support when they felt that it was needed. Furthermore, they were accustomed to collaborating with other professionals and understood the system.

However, adopters in all three groups were anxious to deal with problems without recourse to professional agencies if they could. This theme ran through several of the studies and was closely related to the new parents' desire to 'normalise' the position of their family. Continuing contact with adoption workers could be seen as frustrating this aim. Owen, for instance, reported that some of the adopters in her sample had been anxious to terminate social work visits for fear of resurrecting 'unpleasant experiences' for the child; and there were those who wished to be 'self-sufficient' once the order had been made, an observation which illustrates how the 'demand' for social work support may vary before and after that point. One important factor that influenced whether or not 'the professional world was held at bay' after the order had been made was whether there was continuing contact with the birth family: if there was, help with its management was likely to be appreciated.

Thoburn and her colleagues reported cases where adopters had decided to sever contact with the adoption agency when the social worker who had 'approved' them (and with whom they had formed a good relationship) left. Others, as already noted, were selective in the assistance which they sought from social workers. For example, few turned to their social workers for help with issues of ethnic identity, race or racism. This was particularly true of the white parents who had adopted black children and who now felt reproached for having done so. As one put it: 'It's not our fault that it was decided a few years later that white people shouldn't adopt black children.'

A further constraint upon adopters who might well have welcomed social work help was the feeling that the admission that help was needed was also an admission of inadequacy, if not failure. This could be a particular concern until the order was made. We have seen how preparation and assessment could become confused – but so too could assessment and support, with both children and adopters having the lingering sense that they were subject to critical scrutiny.

Thus, although the studies do not offer a comprehensive picture of the demands that adopters made upon social work services it is clear that these varied considerably and had an effect upon what was provided. It is by no means as clear that the children could or did express their needs for such support, or that they appreciated what might be available. Indeed, in both the Thomas and Beckford and the Thoburn studies it was noted that children had little to say about the social workers. Furthermore, some remained uneasy about visits, feeling that they re-confirmed that their status was different from that of other children.

Support and outcomes

It is reasonable to assume that the better supported an adoption is the more likely it is to be successful. Indeed, that is an important part of the justification for professional assistance. If post-placement services are to be improved and extended, then the consequent additional expenditures will be expected to lead to better outcomes. However, several of the studies make it plain that matters are more complicated than this. In the first place the definition of what constitutes a positive or negative 'outcome' is far from settled. Secondly, if, as the Quinton and Rushton study found, it is the placements which are the most problematic that receive the most intensive support it may be hard to show that 'support works'.

Indeed, Quinton and Rushton found no relationship between the level of social work support and the stability of the placement at a year or with the level of maternal stress. A similar picture emerged from the analysis of the direct work done with the children over the first year: yet again, however, it was the most problematic cases that attracted most of the social work investment. Of course, as the authors acknowledge, it may take longer than a year for the beneficial effects of any of such efforts to become apparent.

These findings suggest several conclusions and raise a number of critical issues. First, it is clear that social workers can and do identify the families and children who are facing the greatest difficulties. Indeed, both CSWs and FSWs predicted quite accurately at one month which placements would pose problems and which would not. It would seem that they then adjusted their 'support' accordingly, although families with problems may also have been more demanding. The implication, however, is that a number of the placements had been made in the expectation that they were likely to be hazardous, and probably in the knowledge that they would require exceptional support. Under what circumstances is it decided to go ahead with such placements? How are the pros and cons weighed, by whom and for whom?

Are the consequences for other adoptive families which may not face comparable difficulties (or which may be less demanding) taken into account? Although they were often satisfied with what Quinton and Rushton classed as a 'moderate' service they might well have benefited from a higher level of support, not least in helping to reduce the strains which, although not overwhelming, made life more difficult than it need have been.

Another important finding from the Quinton and Rushton study was that the extent of adopters' satisfaction with the social work support that they received was not commensurate with its level (as assessed by the researchers). For example, 41% of the 'high level' social work was not considered to have been helpful. In general, this discordance seems to have arisen when the FSWs were concerned about the sensitivity, warmth or parenting styles of the new parents and had taken steps to achieve their modification, a process that could be unwelcome and which could be interpreted as criticism or intrusion rather than support. The challenge of tackling certain unsatisfactory aspects of parent-child relationships without alienating the parents clearly calls for considerable skill and sensitivity, not least when the parenting styles of applicants are being assessed.

Finally, it needs to be stressed that the justification for the provision of social work support is not to be reckoned only in terms of whether it ensures a 'successful' outcome. As Lowe and Murch point out, for example, there is the work that should be done with the birth family; the assistance and explanation that those who are not approved as adopters deserve to be given, and the considerable need for support that both children and adopters have when a disruption occurs. In short, the value of good social work cannot be evaluated solely in relation to conventional measurements of outcome at fixed (and usually fairly short-term) periods. There are other grounds for its provision as well, and it may be that there are some unfortunate placements that defy the best skills that social work has to offer.

The Main Points

The majority of adopters were satisfied with at least some aspects of the social work support that had been provided, although overall about a quarter were not. These discontents could be created early on (for instance, during the home study) and were then liable to colour all that was done thereafter.

Adopters were least satisfied with responses to their need for material help, for practical guidance and advice about managing their day-to-day problems with the children and to the needs of their birth children.

The characteristics of the social workers that were valued by adopters were: their reliability and ready availability, their wise counsel and their allegiance.

There was no evidence in these studies that the level of formal support affected outcomes. One important reason for this was that it was the more problematic cases which, typically, attracted high level social work.

Social workers identified early on those placements which were facing, and continued to face, the greatest problems. This suggests that these could have been − and perhaps were − recognised before the placement. Going ahead with such placements has implications for the distribution of resources and may affect adversely the service being offered to others.

The adopters' satisfaction with social work did not necessarily reflect its assessed quality. This seems to have occurred when the social worker was concerned about the style of parenting and was endeavouring to engineer a different pattern. The modification of parenting practices once a placement has been made poses a particularly difficult task for social workers and one which would be better avoided by the more rigorous selection of adopters.

Less than satisfactory support may not cause a placement to collapse, but it may mean that the 'costs' to both the children and their new parents are unnecessarily heavy.

The social work support that is provided is not only a reflection of 'supply side' factors but also of those encapsulated in what adopters (and children to a much lesser extent) expect and then demand. The nature and structure of this 'demand' can vary considerably: according to the circumstances and motivation of the adopters; their earlier experiences of social work and particular social workers; the stage the placement has reached (for example, before or after orders have been made); and in relation to the severity of the problems that they encounter.

There is evidence that some adopters refrain from seeking the help and support that they need for fear that in revealing their problems they will appear less than adequate parents. Unless this issue is dealt with honestly, not least during preparation, adopters may not be frank about the support they need.

One of the largely unexplored areas in the studies is the nature of the need for social work support that the children may have at different times and at different ages. They may not be able to articulate that need, or it may be interpreted by their adopters, albeit sympathetically, but not necessarily accurately. Opportunities have to be created for children themselves to communicate their needs.

8

Issues of organisation

The local authorities

Scale

Of the local authorities in England[1] which made returns for 1997[2] 43% had
fewer than 10 children who 'ceased to be looked after' because of their
adoption; 29% had 10–19; in 18% the range was between 20–29, and in only
10% were there more than 30. Only four authorities recorded 50 or more
children leaving care via adoption. Thus, nearly three-quarters of local
authorities had fewer than 20 looked-after children adopted in the year. In the
London boroughs (both inner and outer) the numbers were low, with none
exceeding 14 adoptions. They were also generally small in the unitary
authorities.

However, these figures have to be viewed alongside the size of the
authorities' child care activities. The Department of Health statistics give the
number of adoptions each year as a proportion of all looked-after children on
31 March. In only three authorities did this reach 10%, whilst most of the rest
clustered around the national level of 4%.[3] Although these figures give a sense
of the relative importance of adoption in various authorities they do not show
what proportion of children were *potential* candidates for adoption. This is
important, since most of those who are 'looked after' will never fall into this
category and, in any case, the proportion who do will vary from one place to
another. This is illustrated in the table at the top of page 97 which lists those
looked-after children who will be very unlikely to require an adoptive home.

---

1 No comparable figures for Wales are yet available for 1997.
2 The published returns for 1998 do not include these data.
3 From the Department of Health *Children Looked After by Local Authorities
   (England)* statistics. The number of adoptions expressed as a percentage of all
   'discharges' in the year offers a somewhat better, though still far from satisfactory,
   index. Of course, there are also those children who are already placed for adoption
   but where the order has yet to be made. At the end of March 1998 there were 2500
   such children in England.

**Of the 53300 looked-after children in England at 31.3.98 the
categories unlikely to require adoption on that date**

Looked-after on a voluntary basis	19200
Subject to an interim care order	6300
Placed with parents	5600
Fostered with relatives	5300
Living independently	1200
On remand, detained, etc.	600
Subject to an emergency protection order	250
In prison, youth treatment centre, etc.	250
(38700 is 73% of the total 'looked-after')	38700

Of course, there is a degree of overlap between the categories; but others (for
example, some of those over 16) will not have been included. In any case, this
will be a minimum estimate. Even so, it makes the point that, at any one time,
about three-quarters of looked-after children will not be amongst those for
whom an adoptive family may be needed.

Lowe and Murch collected data from the local authorities about the number
of adopters whom they had approved in the last year for which they had
information. Seventy-one per cent of the shire counties had approved 20 or
more families, but only 20% of the district boroughs and 8% of the London
boroughs had reached this level.[4] These 'approvals' offer a further indication of
the scale of local authorities' adoption work. Another is the number of children
placed for adoption in a year. The average in the Lowe and Murch study was
17; the largest number being 79. The Department of Health statistics for 1997
show that on 31 March 62% of the authorities had fewer than 10 children
'placed for adoption'; 23% had between 10 and 19; 10% between 20 and 29,
and 5% 30 or more.

Thus, taking together the national statistics and those obtained by Lowe and
Murch we see a picture of a few large authorities engaged in a considerable
amount of adoption activity but a substantial number of others in which it was
modest or, indeed, very small-scale.

When set against the amount of other family and child care work for which
social services departments are responsible, adoption certainly appears to be a
minor activity. For example, in addition to the number of children 'looked after'
they will be supporting many more children and families in their own homes
(perhaps 1000–2000 in a middle-sized county); responding to child protection
referrals[5]; undertaking the work required by supervision orders, and in

---

4 Readers of the Lowe and Murch study should note that the legend for figure 16 (p
345) is incorrect.

5 For an indication of the volume of this work, see *Child Protection: Messages from
Research* (1995), HMSO.

supervising or checking child minders and private foster homes. Adoption has to jostle for a place amongst the strong claims for priority that some of these more extensive activities are able to make.

Nonetheless, although it is true that in terms of the number of placements made or orders granted adoption appears to be only a small fraction of the workload of social services departments, this does not represent the full measure of either what is currently done or what should be done to ensure a comprehensive adoption service. There are other demanding responsibilities as well.

There is, for example, the counselling that has to be provided to adopted people who want information about their birth families, and to birth parents who wish to find out about their child who was adopted, and sometimes to establish contact.[6] This has been a growing area of work during the 1990s, and one which is far from straightforward. There is also, as we have seen, the exacting work that is generated by the increasingly common practice of arranging continuing contact – managing meetings, advising on responses, running letterbox schemes, and so on. Another demand on local authorities is the requirement for them to provide reports on prospective inter-country adopters. Furthermore, there is also the work that should be done when adoptions break down or when children who are advertised are not placed. There is the counselling of single pregnant women who have indicated that they are considering adoption. Though far fewer than in the past, such cases continue to require skilled help.

It must also be reiterated that step-parent adoptions make up over half of all adoptions. Not all of these are plain sailing and questions about the best interests of the child do arise. Added to which, information for the various reports has to be gathered and in most cases this will not have been previously recorded.

Over and above this variety of adoption responsibilities it needs to be recognised that an adequate post-adoption service involves a potentially long-term involvement in each case and hence that its call upon resources will be cumulative. Moreover, the numerical scale of a particular activity like adoption work cannot be the only basis for deciding its budget; its complexity and intensity have to be taken into account as well.

When all such additional aspects of an 'adoption service' are added up it becomes evident that it is both actually and potentially a larger undertaking

---

6 In 1997 in England and Wales 3230 people were counselled by social services departments; but only 50 by adoption societies; ONS (1999), *Marriage, Divorce and Adoption Statistics, 1996*, Stationery Office.

than would appear at first sight. It is not a small, low-cost or optional extra and this has to be acknowledged in its pattern of organisation and financing.

Organisation, specialisation and priorities

As Lowe and Murch found in both their *Pathways* and *Support* studies, in local authorities adoption is subject to a bewildering profusion of different organisational arrangements. Indeed, they admit that even within one authority they frequently found it difficult to grasp the way in which the work and responsibility were shared amongst the staff. This, they suggest, was partly because it was often 'bolted on to other areas of work' to which it did not necessarily bear much resemblance, especially in the smaller departments. One indication of both the variability and the complexity of its organisation was that those who responded to the researchers' questionnaire in the *Support* study (and who presumably carried some senior responsibility for adoption) bore 38 different titles; and that in a spread of 85 authorities. However, only 10 of these titles included the word 'adoption'.

The *Pathways* study also collected information from the 44 local authority social workers who were interviewed concerning the proportion of their workloads that had been devoted to adoption in the preceding 12 months. It was concluded that for half of them it could not be regarded as a specialised activity since it absorbed less than a quarter of their time. However, virtually all of those interviewed said that 'there was someone whom they could consult if they needed advice and support in their adoption work' and the work of only 13% of them was unsupervised.[7] Nevertheless, the question of whether or not adoption should be regarded and organised as specialist work emerged, the authors reported, 'as one of the major concerns expressed by their respondents'.

How that question is best answered is closely connected with the issues of scale and priority. It seems reasonable to assume that until adoption work reaches a certain volume (whatever that might be) the case for greater specialisation is unlikely to be very strong. Furthermore, in as much as individual social workers remain responsible for other activities as well as adoption, and to the extent that they interpret these as more urgent, adoption work is likely, out of necessity, to suffer a lower priority. However, that will also be influenced by whether an authority has established the priority (and

---

7 Unfortunately, similar data were not gathered in the more recent *Support* study.

resources) to be accorded adoption in its children's services plan or whether it leaves the matter to be settled on an *ad hoc* basis at the local level or by individual social workers. The consequence of this was captured in the words of one social worker in the *Pathways* study who explained that 'something may not be more important than adoption but it may be more immediate ... Adoption can always wait for another day'; the more so, others explained, because once in the care of a local authority a child could be considered to be 'safe'. In particular, as most of the studies emphasised, the priority of adoption stood in danger of relegation when social workers or teams also dealt with child protection.

The *Pathways* study drew attention to the problems that arose from the lack of a standard or co-ordinated approach to adoption work within local authorities (and, indeed, between them and other agencies). These problems, it was concluded, tended to be exacerbated by the decentralisation of responsibilities. Certainly, this was a theme that was also articulated by the social workers who were interviewed in the later *Support* study; but the pros and cons were altered by the extent to which, at the local level, there were or were not specialist adoption workers. Where there were, the priority of adoption activities was more likely to be protected.

One further issue that appeared to affect the priority given to adoption work was the extent to which the efforts of a particular unit, area or authority yielded results that added to or diminished *their* resources. One of the problems is that authorities in more affluent areas may have fewer children to place but more prospective adopters. They may have, therefore, little incentive to devote resources to further recruitment. Such impediments to the expansion of adoption are more likely to be overcome by the payment of inter-agency fees rather than by other forms of negotiation. Even when fees were used (and most authorities in the *Support* study said that they had paid them) there remained the question of exactly what they bought, especially in terms of support after the placement had been made.

The need for some arrangements for pooling was illustrated in the Lowe and Murch *Support* study. They found that in 65% of the local authorities replying to their questionnaire more children than families were approved for adoption in the year in question and in 35% more families than children.[8] Of course, there may have been other children and adopters who had been approved

---

8 Overall (statutory and voluntary agencies combined), the panels of the agencies replying to the questionnaire had approved 2036 children for adoption and 1932 families to be adopters in the latest year for which they had figures.

earlier but who still waited to be 'matched'. Furthermore, even those authorities which had a 'surplus' of approved adopters may not have had amongst them the right family for the children they wished to place. For reasons like these many authorities had become members of, or had used, a 'pooling' scheme.

Lowe and Murch, for example, found that 69% of the local authorities in their study were members of regional consortia (some of more than one); many others were also members of national linking organisations, such as BAAF, and used the *Be My Parent* service. Although these schemes were acknowledged to serve a variety of purposes, the most commonly noted advantage (by 68% of those who had used them) was the increased possibility of matching children with families.

Over and above this, many of the local authorities in the *Support* enquiry resolved the problem of securing the adoption services which they were unable or unwilling to provide themselves through service agreements with voluntary agencies. The information which the researchers gathered indicated two broad patterns: first, the *ad hoc* or selective use of such arrangements, either for particular children or particular services and, secondly, long-term agreements whereby local authorities paid in advance for a special service or for a certain number of placements. The latter had financial advantages for both agencies: the statutory bodies obtained placements at less than the standard inter-agency fee and the voluntary organisations were guaranteed a certain annual income, and thus an element of stability to their budgets. Unfortunately, the study did not indicate the extent of these different service arrangements, although it did imply that their *ad hoc* use was much more common than standing contracts.

The Main Points

The organisation of adoption in social services departments is extremely variable and often difficult for those outside to comprehend. The increase in the number of local authorities following local government re-organisation has complicated the picture further as well as creating more small departments. Adoption work appears to be a minor activity when set against the magnitude of a local authority's other child care responsibilities. However, when *all* aspects of a comprehensive adoption service (as well as its improvement) are taken into account its scale is larger and more diverse than is generally appreciated. Whether in terms of units, staff or functions, specialisation in local authority adoption work was not found to be extensive, although there were notable exceptions. Normally, such responsibilities were combined with other tasks. Where these were deemed to have a high priority adoption was liable to suffer.

> Given the imbalances between the availability of potential adopters and children requiring adoption in particular authorities, resources and needs have to be brought together over a wider area. Inter-agency schemes or consortia will often be necessary; but this will require a commitment to the payment of inter-agency fees. What exactly these buy needs to be clear.
>
> Some authorities will need to enter into service arrangements with voluntary agencies. There is much to be said for these to be standing contracts.

The voluntary agencies

The information that Lowe and Murch collected about the organisation of the voluntary agencies was far less comprehensive than that which they gathered about the local authorities; and it was not supplemented by material from any of the other studies. Nonetheless, there were several important findings.

Scale and specialisation

The adoption activities of the voluntary agencies surveyed (30) in the *Support* study were generally on a smaller scale than those of the local authorities. Indeed, most operated with far fewer resources, both in terms of their staffing and budgets. Forty-three per cent of them 'matched, or had agreed to match'[9] fewer than 10 children in the year for which they provided statistics. A further 39% were involved with between 10 and 19. Only one dealt with 40 or more. The average number on their case-loads was 13, half that of the local authorities.

A similar picture emerged from the information about the number of adopters whom the voluntary bodies had approved. Forty-three per cent had approved fewer than 10 in the relevant year (compared with 26% of the local authorities) and a further 36% between 10 and 19 (the proportion was 31% of the local authorities).

Thus, some of the problems associated with the small scale of adoption work which local authorities faced were also faced by their voluntary counterparts. However, some of them were not engaged in any other family and child care work, and those which were usually operated separate adoption units. As a result, their staff were generally more specialised in the sense that they were

---

9 However, it must be noted that this is a different definition from that used in the local authority data.

more likely to devote most or all of their time to adoption work; indeed, the few who were interviewed in the *Pathways* study had usually spent more than three-quarters of their time on activities connected with adoption. However, in comparison with local authority social workers those in the voluntary agencies appeared to have undertaken little direct work with children and their birth families; their involvement was more with adopters and potential adopters.

Other issues

Certain other findings from the Lowe and Murch *Support* study also suggested that the voluntary agencies tended to concentrate on finding adoptive families for particular categories of children. Although two of them dealt only with babies, in general they were likely to be more involved with the placement of older children, especially those aged from five to nine. Furthermore, minority ethnic children constituted a larger proportion (21%) of the placements made by voluntary bodies than they did of those made by the local authorities (13%). This doubtless reflected the fact that the voluntary agencies had approved proportionately more adopters from ethnic minorities (15% compared with 8%). However, a third of these agencies had not approved any such families in the year in question, suggesting that there was a degree of specialisation in this respect amongst the voluntary organisations.

Indeed, it needs to be borne in mind that, just like the local authorities, the differences between one voluntary agency and another can be considerable. It may not always be appropriate therefore to compare the one sector with the other, but rather to note the variations within them. Sweeping generalisations about *the* voluntary sector or *the* local authorities are likely to be misleading. It is also important to recognise the dependence of the former upon the latter: for referrals and for the accompanying fees. This is likely to influence their policies. Indeed, the referrals that they received from the local authorities were typically children with special needs for whom it had proved difficult to find an adoptive family.

The Main Points

The scale of the adoption work of the voluntary agencies is generally smaller than that of the local authorities, their average adoption case loads being half the size. Forty-three per cent of those canvassed in the Lowe and Murch study dealt with fewer than 10 placements a year.

> However, the voluntary agencies were more specialised than the local authorities
> in the sense that the work was more often organised around adoption and in
> as much as their social workers devoted most of their time to adoption, albeit
> mainly to work with adopters rather than birth families.
>
> The voluntary agencies are likely to be more specialised in terms of the children
> whom they set out to place: these are more often older than those placed by
> the local authorities; to be from minority ethnic backgrounds, and to be
> sibling groups. These and other differences are likely to reflect the referrals
> received from local authorities.
>
> Problems associated with unevenness in the flow of referrals, and with the
> consequent fluctuation of income, place a premium upon close collaboration
> between the sectors in reaching mutually satisfactory service agreements.
>
> The differences between the voluntary agencies may be as significant as those
> between them and the local authorities. It is unwise to generalise about their
> respective characteristics or merits.

General observations about the organisation of adoption services

In order to judge the appropriateness of the structure of the adoption system
overall Lowe and Murch suggest that three key questions have to be addressed.
Is the structure coherent and understandable, especially in terms of lines of
accountability? Is there a minimum size below which an individual service
ceases to be viable and, correspondingly, is there a maximum size beyond
which its efficiency is jeopardised? Are the skills, experience and knowledge of
the staff sufficient and deployed in the most efficient manner?[10]

Their answer to the first question was 'no'. 'Each agency', they comment, 'seems
to have invented its own structure'. They also conclude that there is an urgent need
to clarify who is responsible for what. With respect to their second question they
doubted 'whether very small operations ... which are not involved in consortia are
best placed to provide the service required by law. In contrast', they continue, 'the
larger and more stable services seem better able to recruit and retain highly skilled
and experienced adoption workers'. Furthermore they point out that issues of scale
touch closely upon questions of economic viability and cost effectiveness. However,
they do not suggest what a minimum viable size might be.[11]

---

10 It should be noted that these questions are similar to those to which voluntary
agencies are subject when they apply for re-registration.

11 Nevertheless, Lowe wrote later that they thought that the viable minimum number
for agency practice was between 15–20 placements a year. Lowe N (1997), The
Changing Face of Adoption: the Gift/Donation Model versus the Contract/Service
Model, *Child and Family Law Quart*, 9: 371–86.

When Lowe and Murch turn to their third question about the deployment of staff they link it with a discussion of 'options for restructuring'. Although they argue for a clearer demarcation between child protection work and child placement they also consider the case for and against the relocation of responsibilities for adoption elsewhere than in the local authorities. However, they conclude from their evidence that this would be unwise. First, because it would separate adoption from other activities which are involved in planning for the long-term care of looked-after children. Secondly, because, if the adoption functions of local authorities were hived off there would be a danger that the option of adoption for looked-after children would be ignored. Thirdly, because such a move would be interpreted as a lack of confidence in the child care service, the repercussions of which would be counterproductive. Finally, they point out that the voluntary sector does not have the capacity to assume all these responsibilities and that any specially created organisation would separate even further the work with looked-after children and their families from the work of adoption placement and support.

Nevertheless, they conclude that there is 'no escape from the manifest need to rationalise the service', albeit favouring reform within the statutory sector, together with a better organised and possibly mandatory system of regional consortia and the more systematic development of contractual arrangements between the sectors.

Similar important questions are posed but not answered by Quinton and Rushton in their report. Would the adoption services, they ask, be better located in the voluntary sector? If they were, what would be the effect of specialist adoption teams operating outside the mainstream of child welfare? Would there be better accountability? Would continuity in the planning of the care of looked-after children be jeopardised? Would the links between CSWs and FSWs be harder to maintain? Furthermore, they point out 'that the work of supporting families with highly disturbed children is going to be extremely difficult' whatever the organisation.

Messages for policy and management

Previous chapters have tended to emphasise the implications for practice that have emerged from the studies. Here the main messages for policy and for management are gathered together in a way that highlights the principal *issues* that require to be addressed at these levels.

Information

Information for policy and management

Many of the projects report on the deficiencies that were found in the recording and collection of basic information; that is, in the kind of routine data that enable governments and organisations to monitor what is happening, to be alert to changes, to recognise shortcomings or to realise that certain matters should be investigated. Even when records were reasonably well kept there were considerable differences between the agencies in their format and coverage.

Accurate and relevant information is essential for the wise development of policy, but it is probably more inadequate in adoption than in any other field of child care. Welcome moves to improve the quality and coverage of national adoption data have been put in train, most notably by BAAF through their statistical reports[1] and by the Office for National Statistics; but the success of such endeavours relies upon the care with which these data are assembled locally. That will depend upon how clear staff are about what information is to be kept, in what format and for what purpose. It will also depend upon the

---

1 See BAAF (1997), *Focus on Adoption: a Snapshot of Adoption Patterns in England – 1995*; and (1998), *Children Adopted from Care: an Examination of Agency Adoptions – 1996*.

appropriate training of the clerical staff who have the responsibility for
assembling these data. If the aspirations of the government's *Quality Protects*
initiative are to be realised then the issue of the accuracy and the relevance of
basic information has to be addressed.[2] An essential requirement is
standardisation. The reintroduction of unit returns for adoption is imperative.
The much more comprehensive statistics of adoption in Scotland might be
noted.[3]

All this is in keeping with the Secretary of State's letter – *Quality Protects* –
that was sent to elected members at the end of 1998. Indeed, many of the
questions which they were advised to ask their officers (and which were set
out in annex B to the letter) cannot be properly answered without good
information.[4]

Information for practitioners and users

The quality of service to the individual is also affected by the quality of the
information that is available. Those who have to make professional decisions
about adoption must possess detailed and accurate histories of the children in
question. This is the case with respect to the decision as to whether a child
should be adopted (and if so when); with respect to the preparation that they
need; to whether they should be placed with their brothers and sisters; to the
kind of family that is most likely to meet their needs; and to the support that is
required to sustain them in the placement and to minimise the stresses and
strains which they might face. Wise decisions about adoption also depend
upon a detailed and up-to-date knowledge of the birth families and of the
families into which a child might be placed or has been placed.

However, what is clearly evident from the studies is that no single piece of
information is of over-riding importance but that it has to be seen in the light
of how it is likely to interact with other factors. Nonetheless, the assembly of
information must be selective and purposeful. Indiscriminate lists of what

---

2 Symptomatic of the present deficiencies is the fact that the number of adoption
orders made in England and Wales in 1996 is recorded in the *Statistics of Marriage,
Divorce and Adoption* (Office for National Statistics FM2 no. 24, 1999) as 5962 but
in the *Judicial Statistics* (Lord Chancellor's Department, Cm 3716, 1997) as 4936.

3 See Scottish Office (various dates), *Statistical Bulletin: Social Work Series*, Adoption
Applications in Scotland, Govt. Statistical Service.

4 Department of Health letter 21.9.98: *Quality Protects: Transforming Children's
Services. The Role and Responsibilities of Councillors.*

should be gathered defeat the purpose. The value of the studies that have been considered is that they begin to identify what exactly is the key information.

Practitioners are not the only ones to need good information. Many of the children in the Thomas and Beckford study felt that they had been denied details about their pasts, as well as information about the adoptive families to which they were going. Although valuable for certain purposes life-story books were not all that was needed and, in any case, some of them were missing or had not been kept up to date. Children should be able to obtain a full picture of their histories, albeit later in their lives. Such a history needs to be kept in trust for them.

Almost all the studies reported a dissatisfaction on the part of many adopters with the information that they were given, whether it was about the child, about court procedures, about the support that would be available, or about adoption allowances. The two main complaints, however, were that there was insufficient information concerning the child's background (including their medical history) and that some information was incorrect. It is hard for adopters to prepare themselves, or to decide how best to respond to children, without knowing as much as possible about them and, indeed, without getting good advice about the prognosis for certain problems.

Although none of the studies included birth parents, some indication of their need to have news of their children is reflected in the material on contact and access. Furthermore, it is the birth parents from whom certain essential information has to be obtained: they cannot be ignored. It is also important that the information collected from and about the birth parents is recorded accurately and objectively. If adopters or the children receive only a negative picture of the birth parents and their way of life, attitudes can be created which prejudice future contact or the child's view of their history and origins.

The Main Points

One objective of adoption policy must be the encouragement of the collection, in as standardised and discriminating form as possible, of those statistical data which are needed to improve the quality of key decisions at all levels of the adoption service.

Adopters, children and birth families also need to be provided with relevant, accurate and balanced information in an appropriate form and at an appropriate time.

Integration

The government's view of the place of adoption within child care policy and practice has been set out on several occasions over the last ten years. In 1987 the circular dealing with the delayed implementation of the Adoption Act 1976 pointed out that 'the full integration of adoption into the mainstream of services for children should help to ensure that the possibility of adoption is not overlooked in any case where it would be in the best interests of a child and that the necessary facilities are available'.[5] Likewise, the latest circular (in 1998) explained that one of its main purposes was 'to bring adoption back into the mainstream of children's services',[6] and this is implicit in the government's *Quality Protects* initiative.

Despite these aspirations adoption remains at the margins of the local authorities' child care services. In as much as its image continues to be influenced by its past, this is unsurprising. Until comparatively recently most adoption work was undertaken by voluntary organisations, and it was only in 1988 that local authorities were required to ensure that a comprehensive adoption service was available in their areas. Added to this, the atmosphere of secrecy that has surrounded adoption for much of its history has tended to set it apart, as has the related assumption that once an order was made, adoptive families should become, and be treated as, indistinguishable from other families.

The fact that step-parent adoption has always accounted for a substantial proportion of all adoptions has also emphasised its private rather than its public face. Furthermore, because it has always been (and continues to be) subject to legislation that is separate from that which regulates most other child care activities, adoption is still liable to be regarded as lying outside the mainstream of this work. Indeed, it is noteworthy that it was excluded from the reforming and consolidating Children Act 1989,[7] and therefore only indirectly incorporated in its guiding principles. As a result, practitioners can find 'planning for permanence' apparently at odds with such powerful messages as those that encourage the preservation and rehabilitation of children within their birth families and the development of 'partnership' with birth parents.

---

5 Department of Health and Social Security, *Adoption Act, 1976: Implementation*, circular LAC (87) 8.

6 Department of Health (1998), *Adoption – Achieving the Right Balance*, circular LAC (98) 20

7 Furthermore, the draft bill to reform adoption law which made a brief and abortive appearance would have maintained the same separation.

Yet the findings of these studies provide many reasons which reinforce the view that adoption should be more closely integrated and associated with other children's services. The first of these is because (leaving aside step- and relative-adoptions) almost all recently adopted children have been cared for previously by local authorities. The decision that they should be placed for adoption is, therefore, usually the responsibility of those authorities and it is they who have to compare the advantages of this course of action with other possibilities, most of which it would fall to them to pursue.

The second major reason why adoption work needs to be placed alongside other services for children and their families is that formal support is plainly required before, and increasingly, after an order has been made. Sometimes social services departments will be able to provide this from their own resources, but there will often be occasions where the services that are needed will have to be obtained from the voluntary sector or from education or health departments. However, for these to be mobilised (on whatever basis) there has to be an agency with the unambiguous responsibility for ensuring that that happens.

A third reason why adoption should be located within the context of other child care activities derives from the need to work with both birth and adoptive families in order to make a success of those contacts that are judged to be in the child's interest. Contact not only obliges social services departments to become involved as intermediaries, and in ways that were exceptional in the past, but also to continue that involvement.

The studies expose a fourth and less obvious reason why adoption should be regarded as an integral part of child care; namely, just as findings about other aspects of child welfare can have an application to adoption so too those drawn from studies of adoption can inform other areas of work with children and families. For example, the enquiries into adoption from Romania add to our understanding of recovery from early severe deprivation and of attachment disorders. Likewise, it should be remembered that several of the studies in this review reach their conclusions from mixed samples of adoptive and permanent foster care placements.

Finally, until adoption ceases to be regarded as a marginal activity in the child care work of local authorities it is in danger of being accorded a low priority in at least two respects. First, in regard to the allocation of resources (whether for staffing, training, the payment of inter-agency fees or work-loads) and, secondly, in terms of the options that are considered for the care of looked-after children. Certainly, the inclusion of adoption in local authority children's services plans is a welcome step but, as the Social Services

Inspectors' report noted, only one of the six authorities they visited in 1996 had highlighted it in these documents.[8] However, there is now another opportunity for the position of adoption to be clarified in local authorities' strategic plans, for example by incorporating budgets for post-adoption provision.

The Main Points

Adoption needs to be better integrated into the mainstream of child care, and into planning both for the individual child and for the overall deployment of resources.

If adoption is to be treated as an integral part of child care practice and policy the true extent of the need for the continuing support of children and adopters, as well as birth parents, will have to be recognised. This will be hindered whilst some advocates of adoption entertain out-dated notions of what it entails, not least the belief that the granting of an order is the signal for services to be curtailed or withdrawn.

Specialisation

Dividing the work

While policies need to encourage the integration of the adoption service within child care it is also important for it to be recognised that there is a parallel need for specialisation. Several of the studies showed that one of the reasons for adoption's marginal position was that the social workers who carried responsibility for the work were frequently involved with other child care activities which laid prior claim to their time and attention, especially child protection duties. Indeed, one of the main differences between the statutory and the voluntary agencies was the proportion of their time that individual social workers devoted to adoption.

If adoption is to be accorded its fair share of attention in child care planning and practice then it follows that the social workers involved must be in a position to do so. This supports the case for the separation of responsibility for adoption from that for child protection, although not necessarily from other more closely related work which does not command such an overriding priority. In this respect it should be noted that the latest (1998) government circular on

---

8 Department of Health, Social Services Inspectorate (1996), *For Children's Sake: an SSI Inspection of Local Authority Adoption Services.*

adoption makes it clear that senior managers are expected to 'ensure that responsibilities for child protection are not carried out at the expense of children awaiting families'.[9]

However, the issue of the separation of functions also touches upon the fact that two social workers are normally involved in each adoption – the so-called child's social worker and the family's social worker. Although the latter usually devote more of their time to adoption work, the former are involved in more aspects of an adoption, most notably preparing and supporting the child; writing schedule 2 reports for the courts; working with the birth families; and managing any subsequent contacts. The studies found that this pattern of dual responsibility worked reasonably well; but children and adopters did not necessarily know to which of the social workers to turn when their respective duties were not made clear. Nevertheless, because of the rather different orientation that each needs to have it would seem appropriate that the two roles should continue to be distinguished. Indeed, the Quinton and Rushton report suggests that there may be instances where it would make sense for the child to have a social worker separate from both those working with the birth and adoptive parents.

It is, of course, important to distinguish between specialisation and expertise. The one does not necessarily follow from the other, although the accumulation of experience that specialisation permits may lead to greater expertise. Even so, the studies suggest that some of the particular expertise that is required in order to secure a high quality adoption service will not be created simply by a greater concentration of the work in fewer hands. Other initiatives need to be taken.

Working with children[10]

There is clearly a need for social workers to acquire more skill in direct work with children. Many of those interviewed in the studies readily acknowledged the lack. This has to be remedied if children's views are to be elicited; if they are to be helped and supported effectively; if they are to understand their past and present situations; and if they are to be encouraged to fulfil their potential. Indeed, if the aims of the government's *Quality Protects* initiative

---

9 *Op. cit., Adoption – Achieving the Right Balance.*

10 See ch. 6 Triseliotis J, Shireman J and Hundleby M (1997), *Adoption: Theory, Policy and Practice,* Cassell, for an overview of the issues in direct work with children.

are to be met, the development of more skilful direct work with children, and the time in which to do it, is essential. The growth in the emphasis upon social workers as 'care managers' has probably encroached upon what time there is.

The need for such work to be improved is lent additional force by the evidence from several of the studies that adoption workers were prone to become engaged with the adults involved rather than with the children and, furthermore, that these adults were liable to assume that they understood a child's needs and could represent their wishes. That was not necessarily so.

Dealing with difficult behaviour

The research also indicates a second area where greater skills are urgently needed, skills which will not be improved simply by the reshuffling of responsibilities. Many of the adopters who were interviewed sought more and better practical advice about how to manage difficult and disruptive behaviour or, more fundamentally, about how they should help the child towards greater stability. This suggests that at least two initiatives are required. First, social workers need to be better equipped to give such advice or to know how and from whom it could be obtained. That implies a second and, arguably, more important initiative. Steps need to be taken to strengthen, and make more readily available, child and adolescent mental health services, both for consultation and for the provision of therapy.[11] There is a limit to what can be expected of social workers or adopters.

However, neither of these initiatives is needed exclusively in connection with adoption. Much the same recommendations could be made with regard to the problems faced by teachers, by nursery nurses, by residential care staff or by foster carers, all of whom have to respond to the difficulties created by some children who behave in a disruptive and perplexing fashion. It is crucial that, at the policy level, the full extent and implications of emotional and behavioural disturbance (some of which will be clinically symptomatic) is acknowledged and that steps are taken and priorities set to address the problem.

---

11 See Health Advisory Service (1995), *Child and Adolescent Mental Health Services*, HMSO; and Department of Health (1998), *Modernising Mental Health Services*.

Special training

Of course, there are many other skills upon which a high quality adoption service depends that range from the preparation of concise and accurate reports for the courts to encouraging the modification of parenting styles where these are proving to be counterproductive. Yet few of the social workers or solicitors seen in the studies had received any special training in adoption work. Clearly its increasing complexity calls for that to be remedied, both in initial social work education and by subsequent in-service training and through skilled and knowledgeable supervision. Opportunities exist in the current reconsideration of social work training and in the introduction of pilot schemes for post-qualifying courses to improve the preparation of social workers at both these levels.

However well trained and experienced social workers may be they still require the time to apply that expertise. The final observation in the Quinton and Rushton report reaches the heart of the problem. The authors write that 'there is a major question as to whether the current system allows for sufficiently intensive intervention. Case load size and other demands can frequently result in only low level support which may have too little impact to counteract the risks'.

The Main Points

Together with the need for adoption to become an integral part of the child care services, the *particular* demands that it makes upon professional experience and skill also have to be recognised. This argues for the number of different responsibilities that many adoption workers are expected to shoulder to be reduced.

There are identifiable needs for training, most notably for working directly with children, for making skilful assessments and for advising about the practical problems of managing disturbed behaviour. The latter need, however, cannot be met by social work alone: a more readily available and strengthened mental health service is also required.

Consistency

Variation

The variation in practice and provisions was one of the notable features of the findings that the studies produced, findings that were echoed in the SSI report on adoption services[12] and highlighted in the government's most recent circular. Although it admitted that 'variations in the delivery of services are not always a bad sign', it is also emphasised that 'they should be minor and limited to local circumstances and need'.

Those studies which covered a number of agencies (including courts) certainly found wide geographical variations which could not obviously be justified. An adoption service should reach a reasonably consistent standard and provide a reasonably similar range of services from one area to the next. Some of the variations which the studies reported appeared to be attributable to differences in local policies, but others seemed to arise from differences in practice which owed little to policy directives.

'Same-race placement'

The issue that has recently attracted most attention with respect to local authority policies is what has come to be referred to as 'same-race placement'. Although there appears to be a widespread acceptance in the regulations and guidance that children are best placed with families whose ethnicity and culture resemble their own, disagreement persists about how this is to be interpreted and about what grounds there might be for exceptions to be made.

The difficulty of interpretation arises from the large number of variations that there can be in both a child's ethnic and cultural heritage and in that of prospective adopters. The uncertainties that this creates can be partly avoided if it is not considered essential for there to be close 'matching' as long as a child whose race or ethnicity is liable to expose them to racism is placed with people who are likely themselves to have experienced negative discrimination. Such people should be especially well placed to appreciate the nature and effect of these experiences on children and thus to support them in an understanding and relevant fashion. However, if a child's sense of identity is considered to depend on their close acquaintance with their cultural and ethnic heritage, such an 'approximation' would be insufficient, and the search for appropriate adopters would have to be that much more exacting, and include the consideration of religious affiliation.

These issues apart, there is yet another problem of interpretation; namely, the determination, in some cases, of exactly what a child's heritage is. For example, both the Quinton and Rushton and the Thoburn studies drew

---

12 *Op. cit., For Children's Sake.*

attention to the substantial proportion of mixed-parentage children amongst those from minority ethnic backgrounds in their samples; to the fact that not all siblings who needed to be placed together shared the same backgrounds, and to the additional fact that the original ethnic and cultural heritages of some of the children were in the distant past and may have been superseded by other influences. This emphasises the complexity of the assessments that have to be made once these go beyond a simple 'black children to black families' formula.

The weight of the evidence assembled in the Thoburn study led the authors to conclude 'that the requirement of the Children Act 1989 ... to seek to place children with parents of a similar cultural and ethnic background provides a sound basis for policy'. However, they go on to write that such a policy 'has to be applied in the context of detailed information ... about each child's history, current circumstances and attachments, as well as the expressed wishes of the young people, their parents and carers. When this is done', they continue, 'there will be a small minority of cases where placement with, or remaining with, a family of a different ethnic origin ... will be the appropriate placement choice'. Nevertheless, they also stress that this should be based on specific reasons in individual cases. In short, their message is that there should be room for *justifiable* exceptions to be made to the general policy injunction.

The fact that, as the Thoburn research found, black or mixed-parentage children had become attached to their white adoptive parents is not in itself a conclusive argument for departing from the policy that children should be found ethnically compatible families with respect to *new* placements; nor is the fact that, judged against the particular outcome criteria and time scales that were applied, no significant difference was detectable between cross-cultural and convergent placements. There are other questions – of identity; vulnerability to racism and the lifetime implications once young people have left the adoptive home – to be considered as well.

Of course, it cannot be denied that each case should be treated on its merits, whether with reference to ethnicity or other aspects of placement; but such discretion has to be exercised within a framework of policy about what is normally expected. This is what the current guidance from central government, as well as the principles of the Children Act 1989 provide. However, the question arises as to how far these policy injunctions are observed in practice, and in particular, how far the reasons for failing to do so are analysed and justified. Justification may prove difficult to establish where a sequence of previous decisions (and non-decisions) has created the circumstances which then become a *fait accompli*; for example, when white foster carers apply to adopt a black child for whom they have cared for several years.

However, in general (apart from the Thoburn study, the results of which reflect practices that were prevalent more than a decade ago) the studies suggest that there were comparatively few departures from the policy of placing minority ethnic children with broadly compatible families; but, of course, only a limited number of agencies were involved and in some cases (such as the Lowe and Murch study) there were few placements of such children. Nonetheless, the BAAF study of adoptions from care in 1996 drew similar conclusions; namely, that 'in the context of permanent placements, the practice of the majority of agencies, both statutory and voluntary, concerning ethnicity is in keeping with the spirit of the Children Act'.[13]

The spirit of the Act is contained in the requirement that local authorities should give 'due consideration to the child's religious persuasion, racial origin and cultural and linguistic background' in any decisions that are made about them.[14] Certainly, the black children in the Thoburn study who gave their views endorsed the underlying principle of ethnic compatibility in placement choices. However, the Romanian adoption research team express concern that a strict adherence to 'ethnic matching' would condemn all inter-country adoption, despite the fact that the placements in their study (up to the age of six) have been remarkably successful.

Post-adoption service

It is now accepted that local authorities have a duty to provide a post-adoption service, although some legal ambiguity remains, an ambiguity that was more pronounced in the past. As recently as 1993 the government's aim was no more than to 'encourage' post-adoption support, and then only to 'new families'[15];

---

13 However, this is at odds with the findings of the SSI survey which collected data about children placed for adoption or adopted in selected authorities between April 1995 and March 1996. There it was found that 53% of the children from minority ethnic backgrounds had been placed with white families. Department of Health, Social Services Inspectorate (1997), *For the Children's Sake: Part 2. An Inspection of Local Authority Post-Placement and Post-Adoption Services.*

14 See, for example, Children Act 1989 (1991), Guidance and Regulations, vol. 3, *Family Placements*, HMSO and letter C1(90)2, *Issues of Race and Culture in the Family Placement of Children*, Social Services Inspectorate.

15 Department of Health, Welsh Office, Home Office, Lord Chancellor's Department (1993), *Adoption: the Future*, Cm 2288, HMSO.

but, by 1998, it was clearly stated that this was a *requirement* of the Adoption Act 1976. Given the earlier statement it is not surprising that the studies which reported on post-adoption services discovered considerable variation in what was done – and for how long. This was also the conclusion of the SSI's report of its 1996 inspection of seven local authorities. Although some provided a good service the overall quality was found to be 'variable' and 'mainly confined to making arrangements for contact with birth families'.[16]

Most of the studies only followed-up placements over a comparatively short period but, even so, it was found that support tailed off once an adoption order had been granted. Indeed, the studies (such as Owen's and Thoburn's) which drew their samples from adoptions of longer standing reported that the adopters' and the children's contacts with the agencies had not often been maintained, particularly after the departure of the initial worker.

Hence, not only is there a question of the comparability of post-adoption services as between one agency and another but also one about the duration of that support. Certainly, a good deal of support is required in the prelude to the court hearing, but the evidence indicates that the need – both for children and their new families – continues well beyond this point, that it is likely to change in character as time passes and that it is, in any case, liable to be greater at some times than others. A comprehensive post-adoption service, therefore, should be available to all who need it. However, it should be recognised that when adopters or children have had a long period without having had contact with an agency they may not know how to re-establish it or they may be uncertain who to ask for. Up-to-date guidance could be provided from time to time, whether asked for or not.

Naturally, some people will not want to take advantage of post-adoption support, wishing to part company altogether with formal social work services. However, as circumstances change views may change and neither should it be assumed that because one member of the adoptive family seeks to sever contact with agency services others do as well. Furthermore, given the ebb and flow of the need for help and the likelihood of crises erupting, a skilled on-call service should be available irrespective of how recently a placement was made.

There is plainly a need for quality post-adoption support to be equally available and not provided only according to the presumed severity or urgency of a problem. Yet the Quinton and Rushton study in particular showed that high-level services were concentrated upon those families in which the

---

16 *Op. cit., For the Children's Sake: Part 2.*

placements were judged by social workers (correctly it must be said) to be most vulnerable. A post-adoption service should not be concerned solely with responding to 'problems'. Sometimes it will be called upon to furnish information, record and celebrate achievements and successes, or to put a new adopter in touch with another upon whose greater experience they can call.

Policy has to give a firm lead with respect to the provision of post-adoption services in at least five ways. First, by insisting on its mandatory status (something that may need a change in the law). Secondly, by making clear which body is responsible for the service when placements have been made through inter-agency schemes. Thirdly, by stressing the need for its permanent and equal availability. Fourthly, by emphasising that it should be organised and offered in a form that is generally acceptable and, finally, by indicating what such a service would normally be expected to provide. Not only has it to be able to offer direct help to children and adopters but be capable of mobilising the support or advice from elsewhere which it cannot muster from its own resources.

Adoption allowances

One other area of considerable variation between agencies was found in the payment of adoption allowances. Some adopters complained that they were confused about the terms and conditions that applied; and, indeed, these differed from one place to another. There is a manifest case for a simple common system which applies throughout the country. The fact that foster care allowances and residence order allowances continue to be similarly variable, and that there is a need to secure a greater harmonisation between all three allowances, argues for a co-ordinated policy; not least so that foster carers who would like to adopt or apply for a residence order are not deterred by the prospect that they will lose their allowance or have it reduced.

It was not only adoption allowances that varied so much from agency to agency but other cash payments as well. Indeed, one of the areas of the adoption service that generated particular dissatisfaction was the provision of material assistance of many kinds. If a truly broad base for the recruitment of adopters is to be created (one, for example, which does not deter single people or those who are largely dependent on state benefits) then reliable access to compensatory financial and material help has to be ensured and this, at least two of the studies argue, should include paid adoption leave to assist during the difficult period of transition.

The value of consortia and other forms of collaboration

Some progress towards a more uniform and consistent adoption service seems to have been made through various schemes of inter-agency collaboration. For example, those agencies in the Lowe and Murch study which were members of the same consortium were likely to have adopted a more common approach to standards, practices and policy, although it was unclear how far differences existed between the different consortia. Similarly, where agencies had entered into service contracts with other agencies a measure of agreement about their respective policies often had to be reached. However, there were cases where key differences had not been resolved or where one agency (usually a voluntary society) worked with several other agencies whose policies differed. The greater the prior uniformity in agency policies (for example, with respect to inter-agency fees) the more likely it will be that effective collaboration is secured. Policies which encourage the participation of agencies in regional consortia, or in co-ordinated national activities are likely to create more consistency in the services as well as more opportunities for sharing of all kinds and the cutting of certain costs.

The Main Points

Consistency (it may be called standardisation, rationalisation, coherence or uniformity) has to be accorded a prominent place on the national and local policy agendas, the more so now if the objectives of the *Quality Protects* programme are to be realised and if ideas about the establishment of national standards are to be applied. An adoption service should offer a similar range and level of good quality provision throughout the country.

The quest for consistency and the need to respond to each case 'on its merits' does, of course, reflect a tension, but one that is inevitable in any human service. It is especially significant, however, in those which deal with diverse and complicated situations. In view of this it is plainly unwise for policy to be too detailed or inflexible; but it does have to set the *broad* objectives and indicate the principal considerations that should be taken into account in reaching them.

Timing and delay

Delay

One of the themes that recurred throughout the studies was the importance of time. Indeed, several of the enquiries were commissioned because of a mounting concern about the delays that occurred in the adoption process. However, there is obviously a proper pace at which matters should proceed for each child, a pace that provides enough time for the necessary assessments to be made, agreements to be obtained and reports submitted. Furthermore, the right family for a child may not be readily available and, when it is, it will be necessary for the period of introduction to be adjusted for different children. Certainly, the studies indicated that placements could be made too hurriedly as well as too slowly.

Adopters could face the prospect of a long wait until a child was placed with them after they had been approved, and because of this some said that they felt unduly pressured into accepting a child about whom they had certain reservations. Others felt let down, frustrated or ignored as time passed without a placement being made.

There is a good deal of evidence in the studies about how delay – especially unexplained delay – causes uncertainty, anxiety and stress, both for children and for prospective adopters. Clearly, *unnecessary* procedural delay is to be avoided and there are useful signposts in the studies as to what needs to be done to achieve this, most notably the speedier preparation and submission of schedule 2 reports (and in some cases those of reporting officers and guardians *ad litem* as well) and a reduction in resort to adjournments. The research also identifies some less obvious reasons for delay, reasons which raise questions about what is and what is not 'unnecessary' or 'unreasonable'.

Contest

There is an important issue concerning opposed, contested or difficult adoptions (as Malos and Milsom refer to them). Indeed, one of the major changes in adoption has been the shift from agreement to compulsion.[17] This is one cause of procedural delay. Applications for freeing orders, it should be noted, generated even more opposition and delay. Should delays that are attributable (wholly or in part) to 'contest' be regarded as unnecessary? The answer, of course, depends upon the purposes of that contest and upon how far those purposes could be achieved in other ways. For example, both the *Pathways* and the Malos and Milsom reports suggest that for some birth parents the need to contest an adoption springs from their desire not to be seen as abandoning or

17 See Lowe N (1997), The Changing Face of Adoption – the Gift/Donation Model versus the Contract/Services Model, *Child and Family Law Quart* 9: 371–86.

rejecting their child. Were there a means, it is argued, by which, in giving their agreement, parents could make clear (and record for the future) that this was not the case, then fewer applications might be opposed.

It must give some comfort to birth parents to be able to explain to others and to themselves that their parental rights were extinguished against their will rather than with their acquiescence, particularly when the overwhelming assumption is that parents should retain these responsibilities – in full or in part – except in the most frightful and intolerable circumstances. If anything, the potential stigma associated with adoption for the birth parents is greater now than it was when unmarried motherhood was the context within which it occurred. Furthermore, the virtual disappearance of the secrecy surrounding adoption (which was buttressed in part by such establishments as mother and baby homes away from an unmarried mother's home area) has made the invalidation of parental rights more public and more obvious. In such a climate it is understandable that even those birth parents who recognise that adoption is in their child's best interests may seek to counter the opprobrium that they fear.

However, such considerations should not obscure the fact that some birth parents simply do not want their children adopted, perhaps with the hope that eventually there can be a reunification. Similarly, there may well be instances where the plan for adoption is ill-conceived and *should* be challenged. In that respect the fact that the studies which looked at the outcome of contested cases found no instance of an application for adoption being refused must occasion unease, although to some extent this may reflect earlier decisions by the courts which make approval virtually certain.

From the agencies' point of view and from that of prospective adopters there is good cause to avoid parental opposition and this, the evidence suggests, might be achieved through prior negotiations about contact, since adoption with the promise of contact is likely to be more acceptable to birth parents than adoption without. Furthermore, in as much as the prospect of contact reduces opposition it may lead to placements being made sooner and to proceedings being accelerated.

However, the desire to avoid a contest with birth parents may help to explain the reluctance of some local authorities to move forward swiftly with the adoption of certain looked-after children, the prospect of such a contest prompting two specific reactions: a protracted quest for the evidence that will sustain the case in court and a disinclination to abandon efforts to secure a child's rehabilitation with their family. Furthermore, some authorities in the Lowe and Murch survey explained that they hesitated to place a child for adoption in the face of parental opposition in case it led to the prospective adopters (who have to make the application) becoming involved in a disputed hearing, the outcome of which might be the denial of an order.

Adopter reluctance

It is also important to recognise that once a child has been placed for adoption the timing of an application to the courts is in the hands of the prospective adopters. The Quinton and Rushton study in particular drew attention to the fact that where they felt that the placement was not progressing well (in terms of, for example, a lack of attachment, difficult behaviour or conflict with birth children) intending adopters were reluctant to lodge an application, being unconvinced that matters would improve as time passed and that they might well worsen. Indeed, the Lowe and Murch study found that most breakdowns occurred *before* an adoption order had been made. How far this reflected the fact that unwise placements had been made in an endeavour to avoid delay or in order not to keep prospective adopters waiting too long was not explored.

The search for information

As has been argued, the availability of sound relevant information is crucial if sensible policies and sensitive practice are to be achieved. However, the studies make clear that the search for information is one important cause of delay; and that it is sometimes linked with the need to search for the birth parents (especially fathers) in order to obtain their signatures to agreements and to gather certain facts. Even when they are located parents may be unwilling to provide information.

Such problems emphasise the need to avoid the collection of *unnecessary* information and therefore for there to be a clear understanding of what is needed for different purposes, such as panel deliberations, court hearings, reviews, or for compiling a record that can be held in trust for the child.

The Main Points

If unnecessary and counterproductive delays in the adoption process are to be minimised, the reasons for them have to be understood and policies have to be devised for addressing such matters as parental opposition and the repercussions which follow.

> Although there are undoubted delays in adoption procedures, it should not be
> assumed that everything ought to be accelerated. From the child's point of
> view as well as from the adopters' things may move too fast. The appropriate
> tempo will vary from case to case.
> The assembly of essential information is not always straightforward and can be
> time-consuming. However, if there is a better understanding of what is
> relevant and what is not, some of the delay that this causes could be avoided.

Adoption, fostering and residence orders

As adoption increasingly involves children having continued contact with their
birth families, questions arise as to how it differs from permanent foster care
or from permanent care ensured through a residence order. Of course, the
essential difference lies in whether or not parental rights and responsibilities
have been legally and permanently transferred.[18] However, what determines
whether a child needing permanent family care is adopted, fostered or made
subject to a residence order? What rationale or explanation lie behind what
happens?

Thoburn's research casts some light on the answers. She concluded that the
choice between foster care and adoption depended very much on the needs and
wishes of those concerned: the children, the birth parents and the carers. In
that sense these were *negotiated* options. For example, some children were
clear that they had not wanted to be adopted, even by foster carers to whom
they were well attached. They did not want to endanger links with their birth
families or change their name. Others had more pragmatic reasons. Being
fostered rather than adopted enabled them to explain, in an acceptable fashion,
why they were not being looked after by their parents.

Some people had chosen to foster rather than to adopt because they did not
wish to commit themselves to the finality of adoption, whilst those who had
adopted had sought that finality and the security in their role that went with
it. In between, there were those who had set out to foster or to adopt but who
had changed their minds once the child had been placed with them. Some
foster carers eventually adopted the child for whom they were caring, often
when that was what the child had wanted. Others who had had a child placed
with them with a view to adoption had decided to remain as foster carers when

---

18 Technically there is no 'transfer' of parental responsibility. Parental responsibility is
extinguished in the birth parents and created in the adoptive parents.

relationships were not developing as they had hoped or when they realised that the birth parents would oppose the adoption.[19]

By and large those who were fostering or fostered favoured that arrangement, and those who had adopted or who had been adopted favoured theirs. None of the studies which were based upon mixed samples of adopted and fostered children found significant differences in outcomes in whichever way these were assessed, although previous studies have, especially in the better educational progress of adopted children.[20] The major difference in the Thoburn study was that foster children had more face-to-face contact with their birth mothers and siblings than adopted children. There were indications that this may have reflected the rather more favourable attitude of foster carers than adopters to such meetings.

What distinguished adoption from foster care for many of the children was the need to go to court; the sense of security and 'belonging', and the symbolic closing of a sad and painful chapter in their lives. For the adopters the distinction lay principally in the kind of contract into which they considered that they had entered and therefore in the expectations they had of themselves and of the placement. Foster carers saw the contract somewhat differently, mainly because their responsibilities were clearly shared with a local authority. In this respect, an important difference between foster care and adoption seems to lie in the degree to which the carers feel (and are considered by others to be) *wholly* responsible for the child's behaviour or education, for their successes or shortcomings. This may shape the nature of their satisfactions and dissatisfactions.

There are, therefore, differences between the two forms of permanent substitute care that derive from ways in which they are interpreted, from the expectations which they create, and from the consequences to which they are believed to lead. Such differences are not simply reflections of their different legal status, although they may well have been determined by it. Nonetheless, there are also similarities between foster care and adoption, not least in the

---

19 Some children are placed for adoption under the Adoption Agencies Regulations and become 'protected children' until the order is made; although supervised by the local authority these are not treated as foster care placements. Other children are placed with a view to adoption *as* foster children, the placement becoming subject to the Children Act 1989 Regulations until the adoption order has been granted.

20 However, it is difficult to make comparisons because the initial problems of the children may not have been the same in the two forms of placement; but see Gibbons J et al (1995), *Development after Physical Abuse in Early Childhood*, HMSO.

problems that have to be faced; in the support that is needed, and in the relevance of the kinds of research findings that have been considered.

Obviously, the choice of foster care, adoption or a residence order[21] status for a looked-after child needing a permanent substitute family has to rest on a calculation of that child's best interests. This, in its turn, appears to have been closely related (according to the Thoburn study) to judgements about the extent to which those interests were served by the child continuing to have face-to-face contact with birth parents and siblings. The confusion that now arises is because that aim seems able to be met in many adoptions, although there may be important differences in its frequency, location, control or quality compared with foster care. Choices are now more likely to be influenced by the determination of birth parents to oppose adoption and by a child's unwillingness to lose the identity of the birth family, both of which factors have become more prominent because the children in question are older than they were in the past.

> ### The Main Points
>
> The differences between adoption, long-term foster care and residence order status need to be clarified, both to assist in practice decisions and in considerations of policy.
>
> We need to know much more about the processes that determine which options for long-term permanent care are chosen and about the respective strengths and weaknesses of each of them for children with different needs.
>
> As well as the need for the distinctive features of each option being better understood there is also a need for their similarities to be recognised and policies harmonised where that is appropriate.

Inter-country adoption

Only the Romanian study addressed policy issues surrounding inter-country adoption. At the time the children in their sample entered the UK there was a good deal of confusion about how such adoptions should be dealt with and, in particular, about the responsibilities that the local authorities had in terms of the assessment of the suitability of the adopters and their preparation. As the

---

21 Residence orders made under the provisions of the Children Act 1989 broadly replace the former custodianship orders. Parental responsibility is not suspended while the order lasts (up to 16) but is shared. In 1996 in England and Wales 1061 public law section 8 residence orders were made (*Judicial Statistics*).

researchers explain, 'at the time of the applications from Romania there was little time or commitment to adapt the [domestic] procedures to the needs of inter-country adopters'. Many local authorities refused to conduct home study assessments and at first 'private' home studies were accepted by the Romanian authorities but later they were not. Some adopters were then obliged to be assessed a second time by a local authority (and often not as speedily as they wished) before their application could be sent to Romania.

The procedures have now been tightened up considerably and placed upon a more systematic footing. The 1998 circular *Adoption – Achieving the Right Balance* provides a summary of the present position. However, certain issues are outstanding.

First, there is the question of what services adopters of children from overseas should be entitled to receive in the UK. Since they have not been approved for children in the care of an agency various forms of assistance are ruled out; for instance, adoption allowances or other financial assistance. However, they or the children may need and could receive post-adoption support, although very few of the adoptive families in the Romanian study had had any contact with an agency once the order was made.

There is also the second and related issue of how services to overseas adopters should be organised, particularly the home study assessments. Can they be absorbed into the adoption services within social services departments, or is some separate and more specialised agency required, albeit involved on a contractual basis?

Thirdly, there is the issue of ethnicity or 'heritage'. The Romanian researchers reported that some adopters took the view that 'the children in institutional care had no cultural identity in Romania, as they were destined to remain in very poor institutional care for their entire childhood'. For these children there was unlikely to be an alternative family placement within their community, and the only opportunity for family life was overseas adoption. These specific factors, which are not applicable to all inter-country adoptions, need to be considered when deciding upon policy. The majority of the families who adopted from Romania were aware of the importance of the children's heritage and identity.

The fourth issue which the Romanian study points towards is the possible growth in the number of inter-country adoptions[22] and the implications that

---

22 In the UK the number of inter country adoptions was: 1993 – 101; 1994 – 114; 1995 – 154; 1996 – 307; 1997 – 223, and 1998 – 258. Special circumstances account for the sudden increase in 1996.

this would have for the adoption service. As it becomes increasingly difficult to adopt a baby or infant domestically more people are likely to turn to adoption from other countries, a trend that is clearly visible in north America, Australia and western Europe. For instance, 3666 children from overseas were adopted in France in 1996. If this trend is followed in Britain the place of inter-country adoption in the work of the adoption service and in the formulation of policies will become increasingly significant.

The enactment in July 1999 of the Adoption (Intercountry Aspects) Bill will provide a sound legal footing for inter-country adoption to take place as well as enable the United Kingdom to ratify the 1993 Hague Convention on the *Protection of Children and Co-operation in Respect of Intercountry Adoption*. It will also require each local authority to provide an adoption service which includes inter-country adoption.

The Main Points

Confusion has existed about the responsibility of local authorities with respect to inter-country adoption. This has been removed by the recent legislation.
Inter-country adoption raises particular issues about ethnicity and heritage which adopters may need help in addressing, both before and after the order.
Judged against conventional indicators of 'outcome' the adoptions of young children from Romania have been so far very successful, despite the absence of 'preparation' and 'support' from social workers. These are important findings that require further exploration.

The images of adoption: a final message

The complex nature of current adoption is perhaps the single most important message that these studies have to convey. It poses many challenges for practice, for adopters and for the children; but the policy issues to which it gives rise also have to be recognised and their implications appreciated. In the first place, although adoption remains a single legal category it now covers a variety of *social* arrangements, such as the differences between, say, the adoption of a baby by a childless couple with the birth mother's consent; the adoption of a seven year-old who has had a chequered history of care but who still identifies with his birth family; the adoption by a parent and step-parent or by a relative, or the adoption of an adolescent youngster by foster carers with whom he has lived most of his life. In each of these examples there could also be more or less contact with the birth family or with some members of it.

Indeed, the decline of closed and secretive adoptions and the increase in contact has done more than anything else to change the social character of adoption and, in the process, the distinction between it and other forms of permanent care has become less clear. This, in turn, suggests that a more searching analysis is required of the idea of 'permanence' and its associated implications. It too is a complicated notion which studies conducted over short periods of a child's life are unlikely to be able to explore. Furthermore, permanence may have a different connotation for each of those involved and at different times. It may also apply differently to different aspects of a child's life.

The radical change in the social character of adoption also calls for a reconsideration of the rights and responsibilities of all those concerned, including the agencies. These can no longer be assumed to have been settled solely by the making of an adoption order.

Clearly, these are all matters that have to be taken into account in shaping adoption policy and, indeed, adoption law. However, one of the impediments to a balanced consideration of these issues is the legacy of the past. Popular beliefs about the character of adoption lag behind today's reality. That affects the political contexts within which it is considered, its treatment by the media and the assumptions and expectations entertained by those who may be contemplating adopting. One of the tasks of national and local policy therefore must be to bring public understanding of adoption up-to-date. This is vital for the efficient conduct of recruitment campaigns, for ensuring that expectations are realistic and, not least, for the amelioration of those distorting pressures to which government, agencies and their staff are liable to be exposed, especially in the absence of adequate national statistics.

Obviously, opportunities such as National Adoption Weeks have to be seized; but there is a *continuing* need for public education. Greater attention should be paid to how an informed debate around *policy* issues such as those that have been highlighted here can contribute to this. Admittedly, that is difficult when the attention of the media is most readily captured by the fate of individual cases; but this only underlines the need for the complexity of today's adoption to be better understood and its implications acknowledged.

APPENDIX 1

The studies described

Support Services for Families of Older Children Adopted Out of Care

Lowe N, Murch M, Borkowski M, Weaver A and Beckford V with Thomas C
Law School, Cardiff University

The details

This study examined the support services for older children who had been adopted out of care from the time of the decision to place them until a year after the order. The work was based upon enquiries to adoption agencies in England and Wales and to adoptive parents.

For the agency study a questionnaire was sent in the autumn of 1994 to all 160 organisations that then existed and 115 responded providing information about the adoptive placements of 1557 children of all ages for the last year for which they had data. This was followed by interviews with the staff of 45 of them (30 statutory and 15 voluntary) about their policies and practices with respect to adoption.

The family study was also based upon a postal questionnaire sent in the latter half of 1995 to all adoptive parents approved by the responding agencies which, between January 1992 and December 1994 (a) had a looked-after child placed with them for adoption, including foster carers and (b) where the child was five or more when the placement was sanctioned by the agency. Disruptions were to be included but it became clear that some agencies had omitted them from the lists that they provided. In all, 226 questionnaires were returned, a 44% response rate. Subsequently, 48 of the families were interviewed.

Of the 1557 children about whom the agencies furnished information, 59% of those placed by local authorities and 50% of those placed by voluntary bodies were under five. Nine per cent of all the children were 10 or older. Eighty-seven per cent of those placed by statutory agencies were white and

79% of those placed by their voluntary counterparts. Overall, 86% of those who were not white were described as of mixed heritage. About a third of all the children had been placed together with siblings. The disruption rate was 10% amongst the local authority placements and 4% amongst those made by the voluntary agencies although these were minimum figures because of under-responding. The overwhelming majority of breakdowns (94% in the case of statutory agencies and 80% in the case of the voluntaries) occurred during placement; that is, before the order was made.

In the more detailed family sample (of 226) the rate of disruption was 6%. Two-thirds of the families had obtained an order but in nearly half of these cases the birth parent(s) had not agreed to the adoption, although only a fifth had actively contested the application.

Half of the families had adopted more than one child (18% three or more), although most of these represented sibling groups. Half of the families also had birth or step-children and a third had three or more such children. Seventeen per cent were looking after foster children. Overall, 54% of the families had non-adopted children living with them.

At the time of the survey, 12% of the children were six to nine years old (none, of course, was under five); 50% were 10 to 14, and 38% were 15 or over. Nearly a third had learning difficulties and a quarter had special emotional and behavioural problems. Overall, 43% were reported by their parents as having 'special needs'. A striking finding was that 34% of the children had previously been looked after by their adopters as foster children.

The findings

In the broadly chronological order of the adoption process the principal findings from the agency and family surveys combined were that:

- Generally, considerable effort was devoted to recruitment strategies but there was evidence that in some areas insufficient thought was given to the recruitment of ethnic minority families.
- Some agencies did not encourage adoptions by foster parents.
- Few agencies allowed prospective adopters to appear before the Adoption Panel.
- Despite the good intentions of statutory agencies (whose job it is normally to prepare the child) many children were inadequately prepared; for example, not all had had life-story work done and some

were moved without any preparation at all whilst others were prepared in such a way that they remained confused.

- Adopters did not always receive sufficient information about the child's background. A common complaint was that it was not up-to-date.
- The primary responsibility for the child's education and school matters was generally left to the adopters.
- Not all agencies held disruption meetings to review the causes of a breakdown.
- Court proceedings generally caused high levels of anxiety, both among the adopters and the children.
- Although most agencies had a formal complaints procedure, it seemed to be little used.
- There was a wide variation in the provision of financial and practical support for adopters, and many did not know what was available.
- It was common for there to be some form of post-adoption contact between the child and one or other member of the birth family; but its management was a considerable task. The appropriateness of contact needs constant monitoring because children's needs may change. It is important not to overlook the child's possible needs to maintain contact with previous foster carers. Although many families indicated that they valued good supervision of direct contact, not all agencies had the resources to provide it. As far as indirect contact was concerned the agency's role was not always made clear to the adopters.
- Not all the agencies kept adoption statistics and their methods of compilation varied.
- There was a significant variation in workloads between the agencies; for example, three agencies had approved no families for adoption in the last full year of their records whereas one had approved 67. Similar variations were found in approving children for adoption.
- Most agency workers felt that their adoption work was under-resourced, both in terms of money and staffing. Commonly, in local authorities, adoption appeared to be accorded a lower priority than other child and family work. This was reflected in the time that staff were able to devote to making and supporting placements, doing life-story work and developing skills through well supervised adoption practice and through training.
- The availability of good quality adoption services seemed to be something of a lottery, being dependent upon the willingness and ability of individual local authorities to provide the necessary resources.

- There was a substantial degree of variation in the way in which the agencies organised their adoption work which, to the outsider, was baffling. It was frequently impossible to determine clear lines of accountability.

Comments

The state cannot consider its obligations towards looked-after children as being *ipso facto* discharged by the making of an adoption order. A post-adoption service should be made an *express* duty. Likewise, adoption allowances should be regarded as the norm rather than the exception.

The introduction of an *Adoption Agreement* (or possibly a charter) for both adopters and children which sets out the kinds of support to which they are entitled should be considered. Under such an agreement the placing agency would give the adopters an information pack explaining precisely what support was available, including information about adoption allowances and other financial support, and how and from whom it can be claimed; guarantee that the information about the child was complete and up-to-date (and that it will continue to be up-dated) and that it would be clearly explained to the adopters; respect the adoptive applicants' wishes (for example, as to the type of child they are willing to adopt), and to continue to offer support both after adoption and even after the child has left if the placement has broken down. Furthermore, agencies should ensure that adopters (and where appropriate children) understand the nature of the agency's responsibilities and who in particular is responsible for what.

Education is too important an issue to be left solely to the adopters. Accordingly, the current obligations upon agencies to inform the relevant local education authority of the proposed placement should be strengthened by requiring them to formulate, with the adopters and, where appropriate, the child, an education plan with provision for any specialist support that may be required. There is also a need for the child's progress at school to be monitored and, in particular, for all concerned to be alert to the risk of bullying and teasing.

The relationship between the agency and adopters should be regarded as one of partnership. Accordingly, the notion of partnership should be written into the adoption regulations and highlighted in any guidance.

Given the relatively small scale of current adoption work there seem to be too many adoption agencies. There is an overwhelming case for rationalisation and amalgamation. There should be a government review to establish a minimum level of adoption agency viability and to consider the possible reorganisation of adoption work.

The Pathways to Adoption and Freeing for Adoption Provisions
(two reports)

Murch M, Lowe N, Borkowski M, Copner R and Griew K
Socio-Legal Centre for Family Studies, University of Bristol

About the research

The *Pathways* research comprised two elements, a court record survey and a practitioners' survey. The former was conducted in five areas, viz. two urban areas in the West Midlands, two predominantly rural areas in the South West and in selected courts in London. Cases were systematically sampled from all three court levels and were drawn from applications made between 1 July 1986 and 30 June 1988.

The practitioners' survey sought to establish the views of social workers who had written the schedule 2 reports and of solicitors who had been involved in a sample of cases drawn from the court record survey in the four non-London areas. In all, 52 interviews were conducted with social workers, 24 with solicitors in private practice and five with local authority solicitors.

The court record survey

Although the detailed analysis focused on agency-placed children, the research findings provide information about the general pattern of adoption. Thirty-four per cent of cases in the overall sample were step-parent applications; 7% were by other relatives; 48% by non-relatives; and 12% were applications to free the children for adoption. Variations in these figures were found in different areas, in particular those which related to freeing cases and to step-parent applications. There was little evidence of applications being made by single applicants. Three per cent of the overall sample were inter-country adoptions, with a concentration in the London area.

The majority of cases were heard in the county court, 78%, as against 15% in the magistrates' court and 7% in the High Court. The major use of magistrates' courts was in relation to step-parent applications. A striking finding was the frequency with which applications led to an order and the rarity of an outright refusal whether or not the case was contested.

On average, it took about five and a half months from an adoption panel's recommendation to a court application. Freeing applications took a little longer, but it took an average of seven and a half months for an application to adopt to be made in the case of children already freed for adoption. In all cases it took progressively longer the older the child. Contested adoption cases took over two and a half times longer to reach the courts than those which were uncontested. However, the difference was not nearly as pronounced in freeing cases.

In the main sample, 20% of the applications were made in respect of babies and nearly half (48%) in respect of children aged up to five. Sixty-one per cent of the freeing applications concerned children under five, although only 12% of them were babies. Thirty-two per cent of the freeing applications were made in respect of children aged between five and 10. Most (79%) of the applications made by step-parents related to children aged five or over.

The practitioners' survey

A number of local authority social workers said that they experienced difficulty in giving sufficient priority to adoption because it tended to take second place to child abuse work. Another concern was the lack of a standard co-ordinated approach to adoption work. Problems were further intensified when more than one agency was involved since they tended to have different priorities. Many social workers considered that adoption should be undertaken by specialists rather than by those with general child-related case-loads.

Both solicitors and social workers were concerned that adoption was often undertaken by solicitors who had little or no experience of that type of work. Solicitors were concerned about the paucity of information made available to them by adoption agencies and by the courts. Another major concern was the often inordinate time taken to process legal aid applications, thus exacerbating the delays.

Practitioners were critical of the generally poor waiting facilities in courts, and many argued the need for a special ceremony. However, the great majority considered that a court hearing was the most appropriate way to determine even uncontested applications.

Most practitioners considered that, in principle, the freeing concept was a good one, but with few exceptions there was disappointment about how the procedure was working in practice, in particular the length of time that it took. For most practitioners, the delay cancelled out its main perceived benefit; namely, that of enabling plans for the child's future to be quickly settled. However, even with the delays some still thought that freeing was advantageous in that by getting rid of the legal complications it helped those 'hard-to-place' children eventually to be adopted. It was also thought advantageous to the child in the long term to know that the contest was not between their adoptive parents and their birth parents, but between them and the adoption agency.

Open adoption was of great concern to many practitioners although there were mixed views about its value. Some kind of open adoption was thought to be most appropriate for some older children who may have established a bond with members of their birth family prior to adoption. It was considered that birth mothers in particular would benefit from the availability of progress reports about their adopted child. If open adoption was to become more common it was felt to be essential that adequate provision be made for birth parents, children and adopters to be given support and counselling, both before and after the adoption order was made.

Some reflections and recommendations

This research showed that the procedures and processes of adoption can take a long time, sometimes a matter of years rather than weeks or months. Of course, every care must be taken in selecting, investigating and confirming a child's new adoptive home, and the interests of the child's birth family must also be considered. These matters should not be rushed. Nevertheless, the research suggests that there is sometimes a substantial element of *avoidable* delay. This might be reduced by setting time limits for different stages of the adoption and freeing processes.

It seemed remarkable that virtually all adoption applications, whether opposed or not, resulted in the order being granted. With respect to contested cases this raised a nagging question as to whether the system is too heavily biased in favour of the authorities; or is it merely that the preliminary machinery is so thorough that the chances of a birth parent successfully contesting an application have been virtually eliminated?

The study considered the question of whether local authorities should continue to have primary responsibility for adoption agency practice. The researchers were worried by the evidence, particularly from local authority social work practitioners, about the difficulties of prioritising adoption work; by its reported allocation to inexperienced staff who may themselves be supervised by colleagues with little or no adoption experience; by the widely held view that adoption needs a more knowledgeable approach than can be provided; by the evident policy variations between authorities concerning such matters as the provision of adoption allowances and post-adoption support; and last but not least by reports of inadequate clerical back-up and support. One option which should at least be considered is whether adoption work should be removed from *individual* local authorities; for example, by being undertaken by regional consortia of local authorities or by voluntary agencies acting on their behalf.

There is a strong case for reviewing the purpose and function of the court machinery and in particular for examining whether non-contentious cases could be dealt with more expeditiously. One approach might be to divert them from the court system by using an alternative mechanism such as the Registrar of Births, Deaths and Marriages, thus reserving the court for contested or otherwise contentious issues. Whatever approach is adopted the need for ceremony should not be overlooked.

If uncontested cases are not diverted to non-judicial machinery, then the alternative suggestion is that all adoption and freeing applications be commenced in the county court with provision that district judges be empowered to make orders in uncontested cases and to allocate (normally contested) cases either to judges of that court or to the High Court in appropriate instances.

It is not certain whether the courts have a duty in adoption and freeing proceedings to consider making alternative orders under s.8 of the Children Act 1989 (viz., in particular, residence orders). It should be made clear that they do.

Delays and Difficulties in the Judicial Process in Adoption

Malos E and Milsom L (now Bulley)
School for Policy Studies, University of Bristol

The study

In order to identify the reasons for delay in adoption proceedings a comparison was made between uncontested and contested cases, or cases where there were serious and persistent disagreements or difficulties. Basic data were first assembled from the records of adoptions completed between July 1992 and June 1994 in a sample of 34 courts in all six circuits in England and Wales (30 county courts, three magistrates' courts and the Principal Registry of the Family Division of the High Court). This then enabled 14 courts to be chosen which were suitable for the study and from which another sample of 247 cases completed between January 1993 and June 1994 was drawn for more detailed study. However, contested or difficult cases were over-represented in order to ensure that there were enough of them to be able to make comparisons with uncontested cases. Approximately half fell into each category. This sample was the basis for the principal findings reported, although additional material was also gathered from a sub-sample of 67 contested or difficult adoptions; for example, information provided in the reports to court.

The sample of 247 cases

In 238 of the 247 applications the order was granted; two were dismissed and seven withdrawn. None was refused. The agreement of one or other of the parents was dispensed with in 43 cases (18%). A guardian *ad litem* was appointed in 38% of the cases. The lowest percentage of cases involving a guardian were step-parent applications (28%). A much higher proportion was appointed for those by a relative (60%) or for overseas cases (57%). Guardians were appointed in most (92%) of the contested or difficult applications. Contest and difficulty were substantially reduced at the final hearing compared with earlier in the proceedings, often, apparently, as a result of negotiation between the parties with the help of the guardian *ad litem* and/or the social worker.

Delays and difficulties

In order to discover where delays were occurring, the time between the different tasks within the court process was measured. Overall, agency cases were the quickest to be completed (a mean of 29 weeks). Step-parent applications took considerably longer (43 weeks on average). This did not reflect their degree of contest or difficulty, confirming what had been reported by the staff at some courts; namely, that step-parents were given very low priority compared with other types of adoption. The 'contested freeing' cases (where a child had previously been freed for adoption at a contested hearing) were completed fastest (a mean of 14 weeks). Uncontested cases took an average of 31 weeks and contested or difficult cases 47 weeks. Inter-country cases took slightly longer.

The time between an application and the submission of the schedule 2 report was more than twice as long for step-parent applications as it was for agency cases. For adoption by other relatives it was longer still. For all types of adoption the date of submission of the schedule 2 report frequently exceeded the six weeks specified in the Adoption Rules. Not surprisingly, cases involving a guardian *ad litem* generally took longer than other cases because of the likely difficulties involved, and this was reflected in the usually longer interval between schedule 2 and GAL reports than between the schedule 2 and the reporting officer's report being submitted.

There were differences amongst the county courts where the average time taken between the application and the production of a schedule 2 report ranged from 10 to 27 weeks with only three courts having a mean of 12 weeks or less. However, as might be expected, the more complex High Court cases took considerably longer.

The finding that there were often long delays in the production of reports to the courts is of major importance. It suggests that there needs to be a more realistic time allowed for the task, with a way of checking on progress so that avoidable delay is prevented. The pain and difficulty inherent in the process of terminating the legal links of children with their birth parents and the establishment of a secure link with new parents can only be increased by unnecessary delay and undue complexity. Furthermore, protracted proceedings increase costs and consume the time of the professionals and the courts involved.

Contest and difficulty

The main types of difficulties included active contest (that is, where birth parents opposed adoption as such; where they disputed the arrangements for contact, or disapproved of the prospective adopters); the refusal by a birth parent to sign the agreement form (sometimes, reportedly, for fear of being thought badly of by the child); a parent's deliberate avoidance of the agency or guardian *ad litem* because of not wishing to become involved in the proceedings, and difficulty in tracing a birth parent. There were also some instances (mainly inter-country cases) where there were difficulties because applicants had not followed the correct procedures.

Race, ethnicity and culture

Most of the children, the birth parents and prospective adopters in the main sample and in the detailed sub-sample were white British. There were few cases where the child was placed in a new family of a different race or ethnic origin. In step-parent adoptions differences in race and ethnicity only featured in a small minority of instances.

Proceedings were completed more rapidly when children were of the same race and ethnicity as the prospective adopters than when they were placed trans-racially or trans-ethnically. Some agencies had attempted to find a suitable ethnic match even where considerable delay resulted. In a few cases there were difficulties because of different cultural interpretations of adoption.

Difficulties in 'matching' arose particularly in cases where the child was of mixed parentage; where the child had been placed with a short-term foster carer who was from a different cultural background and the placement became long-term, or where the origin of one or more of the child's birth parents was unknown.

Contact issues

The types of contact between the child and the birth family in the period up to the hearing varied considerably: from face-to-face in a minority of cases to occasional indirect communication in many more where contact existed. This often involved an arrangement whereby the child was sent a Christmas card or news of the family and where cards or reports on the child's progress were sent to a birth parent, in both instances via an agency.

Few birth parents who were not in the same household as their children were maintaining contact with them by the latter stages of the adoption proceedings, and there was little difference between contact at the time of the application and at the time of the outcome of the proceedings. There were more grandparents and siblings known to be in contact with the child than birth parents, other than those who were living with them.

A large number of birth parents wanted some form of contact after the order, but the only recommendations were for indirect contact. Cases where the issue of contact with a birth parent was directly linked to the parent's agreement to adoption were rare. A number of grandparents wished to have contact, or a continuation of contact, and this was occasionally included in recommendations in a schedule 2 report.

In the majority of cases, social workers or guardians *ad litem* reported that they were confident that prospective adopters would deal responsibly with the question of contact and the provision of information regarding the child's origins. However, there were only five cases where contact orders were made at the time of the adoption order, and these were all for indirect contact.

The wishes and feelings of the child and members of the birth family

The reports noted that children sometimes had strong feelings about either wanting contact or no contact with a birth parent or a sibling. There were few who did not wish to have (or to continue to have) contact with a grandparent. There were no cases where a child's wishes and feelings conflicted with the recommendation in the GAL or schedule 2 reports.

Most of the children whose views were recorded were said to be strongly in favour of their adoption. The progress and behaviour of younger children in their placements was also reported on positively. However, in some cases children were said to be made anxious by the delay in completing the proceedings.

Adoption by Single People

Owen M
School of Cultural and Community Studies, University of Sussex

In spite of the fact that single people have been entitled to apply to adopt since the first legislation in 1926, this provision seems to be under-used. The BAAF publication *Focus on Adoption: a Snapshot of Adoption Patterns in England, 1995* (Dance, 1997) reported that only 6% of the adopters approved by local authorities and 9% of those approved by voluntary agencies were single. Amongst families in the general UK population, one in five is a single-parent family.

The idea for a study of single-person adoption came from the Independent Adoption Service but the research was extended to include two other voluntary adoption agencies, namely the Manchester Adoption Society and the Thomas Coram Foundation. The research was conducted between 1993 and 1994 and its aims were:

- to document and comment on the experiences of single adopters and their children;

- to investigate the official systems by which the adopters were approved and supported, and
- to make some estimate of the children's progress.

The sample was composed of two groups of people. First, there were 30 adults (28 women and two men), all of whom had contacted an adoption agency as a single person and made a successful application for a child at some time in the last 10 years. Secondly, there were the 48 children who had been placed with them.

Some of the adopters had had partners previously, but only nine had had their own children. Sixteen had professional backgrounds, and 11 women were black. They were all linked with children who were classified as having special needs. Twenty-two children (46%) were older white children from deprived or abusive backgrounds. Sixteen (33%) were black children or children of mixed parentage who were deemed to need a culturally appropriate placement. The remaining 10 children (21%) were physically or mentally disabled.

Material for analysis was drawn from semi-structured interviews with the adoptive parents and with children over the age of six, together with file studies and the completion of the standardised questionnaires from the *Looking After Children* project.

The research showed that many of the adopters had been slow to apply, and that beliefs about the unacceptability of single-person adoption had acted as a deterrent. Over half the applicants who responded to an advertisement were surprised to learn that single people were not necessarily excluded. Some black single women also feared that they would be less likely to be approved than white applicants (even when they were applying for a black child) or that they were likely to be ruled out on grounds of low material resources.

Some of the referrals from local authorities indicated that a single applicant might be preferred to a couple when the reasoning was grounded in developmental psychology (issues of attachment were prominent here). However, it was rare for a single person to be selected as a first choice because of the identified needs of the child. It was more usual for them to be considered after the local authority had searched for a married couple and failed to find one.

For most female applicants, their own mothers had been important figures in their upbringing. Whether or not the grandmother had been a single parent, she had generally taken responsibility for most of the child care. This meant that the adopters had good role models together with clear expectations of what it was possible to achieve. Many of them also felt genuinely sympathetic to the birth mother. As single women, they understood the financial and emotional pressures to which she had been subjected, and they understood some of her experiences at the hands of men.

Forty-two per cent of the children in the sample had a history which included physical or sexual abuse, and in six cases they had suffered both. Nine girls had been sexually abused. All of them, whose ages at placement had ranged from six to 11, valued the opportunity to have a one-to-one relationship with a caring woman. Nevertheless, some single women had adopted boys.

The adopters were not isolated, although some said that they derived their main social and emotional support from friends rather than from family members. Typically, the single parent and the child or children lived in their own separate household but were buttressed by other adults, who included grandparents (in 69% of cases) and siblings of the adoptive parent (in 21% of cases). Sixty-five per cent of the children lived with at least one other adopted child, and these were significant relationships even when there was no blood-tie between them. The fact that all the children in the household had adoptive status, and in some cases came from similar backgrounds, seemed to obviate the kinds of problems that can occur when birth and adopted children of similar ages share the same parent. On the other hand older siblings who were birth children could provide non-competitive support, especially when they were young adults and not members of the immediate household.

Adoptive siblings were added to the families, but new adult partnerships after adoption were uncommon. In the three cases where they had occurred, they had mixed success, one being extremely beneficial and the other two fraught with problems. Most of the adopters had previously decided not to take a partner after the adoption in view of the commitment they were undertaking towards the adopted child.

The 21 children who were interviewed talked about and drew their families. Most of them felt that their family was normal. Many had had only one parent in the birth family, knew other children who belonged to single-parent families, and spoke of the advantages of there being only one parent. Some of the positive features that the children identified were that:

- it made life simpler and more restful;
- the single parent had time and interest to devote to children's activities; and
- decisions could be made without having to reconcile the wishes of two adults, and that this gave greater consistency and flexibility to the family's planning.

The research identified three groups of single adopters who may be roughly described as 'novices', 'old hands' and 'professionals'. Each of these groups had strengths and weaknesses related to their previous experience. However, the main limiting factors in terms of outcome seemed to be the age of the children; their age at placement; the length of time that they had spent in their new families; and the degree of their pre-placement adversity.

There are three clear points emerging from the study:

- Single people deserve to be given special help so that they will not feel 'less eligible' as adopters. Given the needs of the children currently in the care system and awaiting permanent placements these applicants are often uniquely equipped to parent them.
- It makes sense to develop ways of assessing potential parents on a mixture of caring skills and social supports. Marital or partner structure is important, but only as one factor among many. Groupings of adopted siblings also have an impact.
- Adoption leave and adoption allowances are not luxuries; they are necessities. Because of structural inequalities, the standard of living may be particularly low for black single carers and their adopted children. Continuous positive action may be necessary to encourage recruitment and to support these placements.

The study showed that some single people are capable of parenting children with quite exceptional needs. If single adopters are not to be treated as a partially disqualified group, however, they need to be assessed and offered opportunities in the same way as everyone else. The child's interests are, of course, paramount; but if more opportunities are extended to single adopters, the welfare of a few more children may be significantly enhanced.

Joining New Families: a Study of Adoption and Fostering in Middle Childhood

Quinton D, Rushton A, Dance C and Mayes D
University of Bristol and the Institute of Psychiatry, London

The aims and design

This study was conducted in the early 1990s when it was evident that children adopted from care were forming a growing proportion of the adopted

population. It was known that the older these children were when they joined
a new family, and the more behavioural difficulties they had, the greater was
the risk of poorer outcomes. Research conducted in this country by Tizard and
her colleagues during the 1980s had shown that although the level of
behavioural problems was a risk these could be managed in adoptive families
in the context of a strong mutual relationship between family and child.

It was important, therefore, to understand more about what was happening
within permanent families when older children were placed. How did family
members and the incoming child/ren negotiate the tasks of integration into a
new and different family structure? What kinds of behavioural difficulties were
most prominent? Which of these tended to be persistent and which were
associated with particular difficulties for parents? What forms of help were
social workers able to offer and what other supports were needed?

Accordingly, with the collaboration of 18 local authorities in and around
London, 84 children between five and nine years old were identified, for whom
the plan was permanence with a new and unrelated family, with or without a
view to adoption. Sixty-one families agreed to take part in face-to-face
interviews at one, six and 12 months following placement. In addition, social
workers for both the children (child's social worker) and family (family social
worker) were interviewed at the one and 12 month points. Some of the 61 index
children moved to their new placement with one or more siblings. In these
cases just one child in the age range was selected as the focus of the
interviews.

The sample characteristics

The sample was fairly evenly split between girls and boys and their mean age
at placement was seven years five months (range 59–121 months). Most of the
children were white and were placed with white families. Two children had
both parents of African-Caribbean origin and eight were of mixed parentage.
There were varying degrees of precision in matching the characteristics of the
birth parents and grandparents with the ethnic, cultural and religious
characteristics of the new parents. Of the ten children with at least one parent
of ethnic minority origin, half were placed with families who had similar ethnic
backgrounds.

The backgrounds of the children's birth families were characterised by
marital difficulties (57%); poor material circumstances (62%); financial
hardship (62%); major psychiatric disorder (22% of mothers, 13% of fathers);

and alcohol and drug problems (38% of mothers, 53% of fathers). The majority of the children had suffered some form of abuse or neglect and some had experienced multiple abuse. The mean number of previous placements was 6.7 with a range from one to 19. The cases of those who had experienced many moves were characterised by frequent attempts to restore children to their birth families.

The mean age of the new mothers and fathers was 39 and 41 respectively. Only three new families were headed by a lone mother and one by a lone father. The majority were couples who had been living together for an average of 14 years (range 3–25). Thirty-nine of the index children were placed singly, although many had siblings who were placed elsewhere. Most of the singly-placed (30) joined families who already had children at home. The remaining 22 index children were placed with at least one brother or sister and most of these sibling groups joined families without resident children at the time of placement.

Each of the interviews with new parents covered a range of aspects of family life: the behaviour and friendships of the placed children at home and at school; the development of relationships within the family; the parents' assessments of the progress of the placement; the level and type of contact with social workers and other supportive agencies; and the parents' views on their need for support. The level of emotional and behavioural problems displayed by the children at home were assessed using the Parental Account of Children's Symptoms instrument developed by Taylor and his colleagues.

The initial interview with the CSWs provided a detailed account of the pre-placement experiences of each of the index children. This included not only events leading up to their being looked after, but their time in foster or residential care and the amount of work done with them in preparation for their permanent placement. FSWs described their assessment and preparation work with the new family and both workers explained their plans for supporting the placement. At the one year interview they both provided an account of the support that they considered had been needed and what had been provided, as well as their views on the progress made.

Findings

There were only three disruptions during the first year, but it was clear that continuing placements varied substantially in the degree to which the parents viewed the experience as positive for themselves or the children. Overall, the placement was considered successful in the majority of cases with nearly three-quarters of the children forming sound relationships with their new families who reported reasonably high levels of satisfaction.

The parents' free accounts of the behaviours they found challenging or stressful focused on conduct problems or opposition from the children. However, the systematic questioning about behaviour revealed that as a group the children also showed high levels of over-activity. The sample showed little change in their behaviour problems over the first year when considered as a group, although this apparent similarity masked significant changes in both directions for different sub-groups of children. Some showed substantial improvements while the behaviour of other children deteriorated markedly. There was a significant tendency for improvements in behavioural problems to be associated with stable placements, but not exclusively so. There was a proportion of parents who remained committed to and bonded with their child despite increasing behavioural problems. However, the majority of those children whose placements were considered less stable showed deteriorating behaviour patterns.

When outcomes were examined according to different characteristics of the placements and the children, poorer outcomes were found to be more likely for children who were placed singly with established families. A number of factors which were found to predict less good outcomes tended to be concentrated in this type of placement. These included the child having been actively rejected by birth parents, the presence of marked restlessness or distractible behaviour, and parents who found it hard to maintain a warm and sensitive response to the child in the early weeks of placement. The analyses indicated that once these three factors were taken into account, the type of placement ceased to make a difference.

The relationships between the incoming child and other children in the household was one of the major concerns that the parents reported. As might be expected, problems of this nature were more common when children were close in age. However, larger age gaps did not necessarily mean a smooth transition, although there was less likelihood of parents anticipating that these difficulties could lead to a disruption.

Although difficulties at school were not necessarily associated with placement outcomes these were another source of significant concern for a number of parents. Information from teachers showed that the behaviour of many of the children in school was significantly more difficult than that of comparison children, and again poor concentration and restlessness were marked problems. In addition, a number of the children entered their new schools with considerable learning problems that had not previously been recognised. Many of the parents of these children felt that they needed substantial support in securing the educational provision that their child required.

The quality of the contribution of both the child's social worker and the family social worker was categorised and associations with outcome were explored. No statistically significant associations were found for the pre-placement preparatory work, but during the year the most intensive family social worker service was allocated to the most problematic placements.

Overall, the study confirms that, even for highly disturbed children who pose a considerable challenge to new parents, permanent substitute care can result in stable placements for the majority by the end of the first year.

The Adoption of Children from Romania

Andersen-Wood L, Becket C, Bredenkamp D, Castle J, Croft C, Dunn J, Ehrich K, Groothues C, Harborne A, Hay D, Jewett J, Keaveney L, Kreppner J, Lord C, Messer J, O'Connor T, Quinton D, Rutter M and White A
Institute of Psychiatry, London

The various studies forming the overall programme are all based upon a sample of 165 children under 42 months of age who were adopted into the UK from Romania in the early 1990s following severe early privation, and a comparison sample of 52 UK children adopted under the age of six months. The Romanian children were divided into those placed under 24 months (111) and those placed between 24 and 42 months of age (54). The progress of all three groups was assessed at four years of age and again at six. Plans are being made for a further assessment when the children are 11.

The major findings fall into five areas: cognitive development, school adjustment, social development, clinical concerns, and the assessment of policy guidelines.

Cognitive development

Although some deficit was evident, there was very considerable cognitive catch-up among these institutionalised children. At the year four and year six assessments, children adopted from institutions before six months of age were indistinguishable from a comparison sample of early adoptees from the UK, none of whom had experienced deprivation. There was also considerable catch-up among children adopted into the UK after six months, although these children lagged behind the earlier adopted children at both the age four and age six assessments. Importantly, further catch-up was not found during the period extending from age four to six years among the later-entering adoptees, suggesting that the degree of catch-up may be limited.

Statementing and school adjustment

Compared with the normal risk UK adoptees, a far greater percentage of children exposed to early privation have been statemented or have received social, educational or health services by six years and, moreover, a recently completed survey indicated that the rate has increased substantially since the age of six. The extent of such school intervention is inconsistent with the degree of cognitive catch-up, and is a major source of concern for a growing number of families.

Social development and peer relations

What is particularly noteworthy is that, among even the early adopted (under six months) Romanian children, some deficits were found on a range of sensitive developmental measures, including peer relations, atypical and aberrant behaviour toward adults and pretend play. There may be less resilience in relation to social development than to cognitive functioning. This may be an important focus for interventions. Moreover, these early deficits may portend later adjustment difficulties in peer relationships and social adjustment.

Clinical findings

Three types of behavioural problems have been identified. First, a particularly high rate of atypical (rather than simply insecure) attachment patterns was found, particularly among children exposed to prolonged deprivation. More strikingly, there was no reduction in these behaviours from four to six years of age. Secondly, a surprisingly high number of children (6%) exhibited autistic or quasi-autistic behavioural patterns. The suggestion that social deprivation is associated with autistic-like behaviours is particularly interesting because it challenges our current understanding of the disorder. Thirdly, problems of inattention and hyperactivity were also noted in a significant number of children, and this, too, was positively associated with the duration of privation. The three areas noted above indicate not only significant needs for clinical treatment, but also possible special education requirements. Nonetheless, when all areas of adjustment are considered together, most of the children including those entering the UK at an older age are adjusting without major difficulties.

Policy issues

Three findings from the study are directly related to the policies shaping international and high-risk adoptions. The first is that certain risks may have been over-emphasised. For instance, the findings to date provide no evidence that families who might have fallen outside the guidelines regarding intra-country adoption were prone to have a placement break down; to be more dissatisfied with the adoption or for their children to be suffering greater maladjustment. Many families who would have been rejected for the within-country adoption of babies and young children (for example, because of the presence of biological children or parental age), are adjusting as well as the families who met current criteria. The second, equally important, finding is that the rate of placement break down was remarkably low, and parental satisfaction was high. This was the case despite a general absence of pre-placement and early support services. Moreover, many families who did receive services reported that they were very dissatisfied with what was offered. The implication is that there is a need to reconsider how support services (pre- and post-placement) are provided. The third finding was that families were receiving a mix of services, and that there was considerable variation in the types of services received and their effectiveness. Nonetheless, the services that were provided were generally poorly co-ordinated, and few attempts were made at evaluating their effectiveness. One implication was that the kinds and amounts of services provided may not optimise the family's adjustment and the adoption placement.

Children's Relationships in Late Permanent Placements

Rushton A, Dance C, Quinton D and Mayes D
Institute of Psychiatry, London

The design

Previous studies have examined relative *outcomes* for sibling groups compared with singleton placements but this study, in addition, explores the sibling *relationships* of children being placed permanently from care.

The aims of the study were to:

- investigate the location, circumstances and contact arrangements of birth siblings who were not with the placed children;
- study factors influencing social work decisions about the separation, reunion or maintenance of the sibling group;
- examine placement outcomes for individual children of a similar age according to whether they were placed with or without siblings;
- explore the character of relationships between children in different types of placement;
- examine the sibling relationships of children placed together from care in comparison with those of children growing up in their own families;
- investigate the impact of placement on the birth children of the new families, and
- document the level of social work intervention with particular reference to sibling factors.

These data were drawn from a prospective, longitudinal study of children placed for permanence with new, unrelated families. At least one child placed with each new family was between five and 11 years of age at the time of placement. Placements that included a child with a profound mental or physical disability were excluded from the sample. Referrals were received over a 21 month period in 1994–5 from local authorities and voluntary agencies in England who agreed to participate in the study.

Seventy-two families took part in the study. They had 133 children placed with them. The new parents were interviewed about all of the children in their family (including their birth children) at three and 12 months after placement. The family social worker (FSW) and the children's social worker (CSW) for each case were also interviewed at both the beginning and the end of the year.

The interview with the parent included a section on the interaction between siblings, and they also completed a sibling-relationship questionnaire. The CSW interview included questions on decision making in regard to separating or maintaining sibling groups both in the past and present; on the whereabouts of siblings elsewhere and the arrangements for contact between the children. In addition, a group of 100 birth parents recruited from two schools completed the same questionnaire as the sample parents to enable comparisons to be made on behaviour and sibling interactions.

The sample was composed of three groups:

- 19 children placed singly in child-free families,
- 13 children placed singly with established families, and
- 40 sibling groups placed with new families.

Although the singly-placed children were all between five and 11 years of age, the sibling groups included children outside this age range in both directions.

The children's sibling networks, decision making and contact arrangements

There were 32 singly-placed children and 40 sibling groups (varying in size between two and four). Most of the children in sibling group placements were full siblings. In 48 of the 72 placements, children had other siblings, of dependent age, who were elsewhere (see the table below). Siblings who remained with their birth parents were significantly more likely to be much younger children and they were very often half siblings to the placed children. All but one of the 11 singletons who had other siblings in care had lived with them at some point in their care histories but, on average, had been on their own for two years. Sibling groups tended to have been together for most of their time in care.

The decisions made about the permanent placement maintained previous constellations in 80% of the cases. Singleton, rather than sibling group placements, had received greater consideration in previous placement choices and in the extent to which a comprehensive sibling assessment had been

Placed children and siblings elsewhere

Placement type	No other siblings < 17	Siblings with birth family	Siblings in care elsewhere	Siblings with birth family and in care	Total
Singly-placed child	8	13	6	5	32
Sibling group	16	11	9	4	40

undertaken. The factors most often mentioned as influential in the decision-making process were the relationship between the siblings; the individual needs of the children; their shared history; and the reports from their carers. A full sibling assessment was carried out in only 16 of 48 cases where there was more than one child in care. Sibling assessments had not been carried out in any of the cases described as unstable at the end of the year.

Just over half (58%) of the new parents of children who had siblings placed elsewhere reported some face-to-face contact with them during the first year of placement. In two-thirds of cases the contact was described as having had a positive effect on the child/ren. On the whole sibling contact was not hard for families to manage, only eight of 26 reported any significant difficulties.

Placement outcome and placement type

Of the 32 singleton placements, 26 (81%) were reported to be stable at the end of the first year, two were in difficulty and four had disrupted. Thirty-six of the 40 sibling group placements (90%) were satisfactory, two were intact but unstable and two had disrupted. Thus, the sibling placements had a slightly better outcome than the singletons, but not significantly so.

Based on the stability of the placements at the end of the first year, social workers appeared to be making the right decisions about placement patterns for the children in their care. Where changes in the constellation did occur it was more likely to be a reunion than a separation. Where children were reunited (six cases) or separated (two cases) the placements were reportedly stable at the end of the first year. Of the 16 cases where separation was considered and dismissed two were in difficulty at the end of the year and two had disrupted. Of the seven cases where reunion had been resisted six of the placements were going well.

Sibling interactions

Both in interview and in their responses to the questionnaire, the parents reported high levels of conflict and rivalry among placed sibling groups, and many felt that the children showed little warmth towards each other. Over the course of the year warmth improved and conflict decreased a little, but it remained substantially higher than in the control group. In some cases these disputes between the children could be incessant and extremely worrying, including a minority of siblings who would regularly inflict injury and some who would need to be physically separated from fights. The severity of disputes was significantly associated with the level of strain reported by the parents at the end of the year.

For new sibling relationships, that is those groups involving a placed child joining existing birth children, warmth between the new child and the others tended to be lower throughout than that shown by children in the control group, although it increased over the year. Levels of conflict or dispute were also low in comparison with the control group but rivalry was high and persistent and on a par with that shown amongst placed sibling groups. Whereas rivalry among placed siblings tended to manifest itself in an overt and physical manner, jealousies tended to be expressed in less dramatic ways within new sibling groups.

The impact on birth children

At both interview points, three and 12 months after placement, parents were asked what impact the placement had had on their own children and how they had adapted to their new siblings. At the first interview, new parents described the placement as having had little negative effect for 10 of the 28 birth children, minor adjustment problems were described in a further 12 cases and more significant problems in six cases. This amounted to 64% who were experiencing some kind of adjustment difficulty. At one year (with losses to the sample) the new parents described adjustment difficulties for 67%. In nine cases these were considered to be relatively minor hiccups which were discussed in the context of the placement having had a primarily positive impact, but there were more significant difficulties for seven young people.

Social work intervention and siblings

The social workers were clearly faced with difficult decisions in making the placement plan and in deciding what action to take if the plans were not working out well. This suggests that social workers need to think beyond received imperatives about placement policy and consider what specific features justify the placement plan. They need to bear in mind the *quality* of the sibling relationships and have at their disposal the concepts to describe and assess the nature of interactions and to think through *the relationship consequences* of decisions. The capacity to be alert to and to recognise relationship problems is essential if social workers are to have a better grasp of the range of challenges confronting the new parents.

Permanent Family Placement for Children of Minority Ethnic Origin

Thoburn J, Norford L and Rashid S
School of Social Work, University of East Anglia

The study provides information about children of minority ethnic origin placed with adoptive or permanent foster families. It explores the experiences of children in ethnically matched placements as well as those placed trans-racially in the hope of improving the selection and support of substitute parents and thus reducing rates of breakdown.

The samples and their characteristics

The 297 children of minority ethnic origin were mainly drawn from a larger cohort of 1165 children placed with adopters or permanent foster parents between 1979 and 1986 (Thoburn J (1991), Evaluating Placements and Survey Findings and Conclusions, in Fratter J *et al, Permanent Family Placement,* Barnardos). Around a third of the placements were in foster families and two-thirds in adoptive placements (although some were not actually adopted). Seventy-one per cent were placed with white parents and the others in families where at least one parent was of a similar ethnic origin to the child. Descriptive data on the full cohort of 297 children and information on breakdown and legal status were collected from records 10 years after placement. Detailed interviews focusing on process and outcome were conducted between 12 and 15 years after placement with 38 sets of parents of 51 young people and with 24 of those young people themselves.

The full cohort and the interview sample were similar in terms of the children's ages and the degree of difficulty they might, in the light of earlier experiences, be expected to present. However, placements that broke down are under-represented in the interview sample since, in consultation with agency workers, it was decided that those which disrupted within two years of the placement would be excluded. The 51 interview cases were also selected so that at least half of the placements were with families in which at least one parent was of minority ethnic origin. Thus these families were over-represented when compared with the full cohort.

A third of the 297 children in the full cohort had two African-Caribbean birth parents; 25% had an African-Caribbean father and a white/European mother; 10% had an Asian father and a white/European mother; 7% had two Asian parents, and 5% had an African father and a white/European mother. The rest had parents of other ethnic origins, reflecting the diversity of ethnic backgrounds subsumed under the description of 'mixed-race parentage'. Sixty-two per cent were boys and 38% girls. Sixty-six per cent were placed alone and 34% with a full or half sibling.

The many gaps in the information about the birth parents reflected the generally poor standard of recording about birth families. The information that was available tended to portray them in a negative light, and there was very little about their strengths, aptitudes or personal characteristics.

Around half of the children had a history of deprivation or abuse, had experienced multiple moves or had emotional or behaviour problems. Over a third were described as showing some features of 'institutionalisation' and about a quarter had had a previous placement that was intended to be permanent but which had broken down.

A minority were either infants or young children with disabilities placed for adoption at the request of a parent, but most were placed past infancy and against the wishes of at least one parent. A quarter were said to need to remain in contact with a birth parent and possibly also other family members, and a quarter to remain in contact with a sibling placed elsewhere. Thirty-four per cent of the children had some contact with one or both parents after placement, 22% had contact with siblings placed elsewhere but with no other birth relatives, and 9% had contact with relatives and possibly siblings but not with birth parents.

A substantial minority of the older children placed from residential care had lived in mainly white environments. Some of the parents and young people interviewed described how they had arrived in their new families having sought to give themselves a white identity, or been harmed by the experience of racism.

The cohort of 297 children

At least 24% of the placements in the larger sample had broken down, including 16% in which the child had returned to local authority care and 4%

in which they had gone back to live with their birth parents during the 10 years since their placements. It should be noted that some of the 80 young people whose placements had disrupted (in the sense that they left the placement earlier than planned) had retained contact with their adoptive or foster parents. Indeed, there was information from the interviews that relationships sometimes improved when the young people were in their twenties. The return to their birth parents could also sometimes be a positive outcome. The breakdown of a placement is not always wholly negative nor does its survival necessarily indicate success.

Four factors were significantly associated with disruption when other variables were held constant. These were:

- the child having had a history of deprivation or abuse prior to the placement;
- the child being older at the time of placement, with 47% of those aged 10 to 12 breaking down and 30% of those who were between the ages of five and eight;
- the child having behavioural or emotional difficulties at the time of placement, and
- the child being described as 'institutionalised'.

There was no statistically significant association between family variables and disruption, including whether or not the placement was 'matched' or 'trans-racial'. Nor was there a significant difference, when age at placement was held constant, between foster and adoption placements. Likewise, contact with birth relatives was found to be neutral with respect to disruptions.

There were few differences between the children placed with two white parents, with families where both parents (or the single parent) were of minority ethnic origin and mixed-partnership families. Each of these three groups had taken a similar proportion of the children who were likely to experience difficulties. However, there was a trend (which did not reach statistical significance) for the children placed with families where both parents (or the single parent) were black to be older; to carry forward into the new placement complex relationships with birth relatives and previous carers, and in some cases to have poor self-esteem and confused ethnic identities resulting from previous placements in mainly white neighbourhoods or residential settings.

The interview sample

The rich material obtained from the interviews with both the young people and their parents threw additional light on the findings from the full cohort. It was also important because experiences and feelings could be heard at first hand and recorded in the words of those involved.

Seventy-two per cent of these placements in this smaller sample had been successful in most respects. However, the young person had gained at least something from the placement in a further 20% of cases, even though important needs had not been met. Only four of the 51 could be regarded as having been completely unsuccessful. On the other hand, our conclusion that only 61% of these young people could be considered as being of at least average well-being demonstrates that it cannot be assumed that early harm will be reversed even by very loving, competent and stable parenting. More importantly, it shows that whilst placement breakdown is fairly unusual for children placed under the age of five, this may conceal a less optimistic picture in terms of their well-being.

The words of the young people and the parents were used to elaborate the ratings which were made for self-concept, self-esteem, racial and adoptive identity. The picture they present is complex. Most of those who were in their twenties appeared to have constructed a sense of themselves as adopted or fostered young people and members of a particular ethnic group with which they were at least fairly comfortable. Those who were still teenagers were mostly working hard, with signs of success, at putting together a narrative which included their complex identities. They had devised different and changing strategies. Some concentrated on getting on with being teenagers and getting a good education, deferring serious consideration of adoption and their first families but knowing that at some time they would come back to what they recognised to be important parts of their identities. Others – mainly those placed with white families – did the same for issues of race and cultural heritage. For some, one or other of these 'differences' or both were prominent in their minds throughout their childhood and teenage years, and had to be dealt with, sometimes in ways which appeared to be harmful and destructive, before they could allow family members or friends to become close to them or develop their educational potential. For another group, mainly those in touch with their families of origin and living with or associating daily with those of similar ethnic background, their growing-up period was one when they were constantly working towards integrating the different parts of their identities. They tended to have fewer calm periods than those in the more closed adoptions but they also avoided the dramatic spells of turbulence or the depressions which occasionally overwhelmed some of the children as they moved through their teenage years.

Implications for policy and practice

The findings in respect of these young people of minority ethnic origin are similar to those in earlier studies of predominantly white populations. Substitute family placement for children in care is hazardous. In this, as in previous studies, child-related factors or early experiences had the biggest impact on whether or not the placement lasted as needed. Neither policy nor practice variables (such as whether the placement was for adoption or fostering), nor family-related variables (such as the age or marital status of the substitute parents or, more central to our study, whether the new parents were of a similar or different ethnic background to the child) were significantly associated with placement breakdown. Some very experienced parents of all ethnic groups struggled and sometimes failed to turn around the lives of some very damaged young people. Others in all groups succeeded with children who appeared equally needy. The data from the detailed interviews do, however, support the view that parents of different ethnic origin to the child have additional problems to overcome as they nurture and guide the child towards maturity. Despite the best endeavours of their parents, some of the trans-racially placed children suffered additional stress as a result of losing contact with their racial and cultural origins as well as with their birth families.

Thus, whilst some white families can successfully parent children who are of a different ethnic origin from themselves, they have extra obstacles to surmount in ensuring that the young people have a positive sense of themselves as members of a particular ethnic group. The requirement in the Children Act 1989 to seek to place children with parents who are of a similar cultural and ethnic background and who can also meet their needs provides a sound basis for policy. Placement with a family of a different ethnic and cultural background should be unusual and should be based on specific reasons in individual cases.

Adopted Children Speaking

Thomas C and Beckford V with Murch M and Lowe N
Law School, University of Cardiff

This is a qualitative study which aimed to contribute to the development of knowledge and understanding of children's views and experiences of the adoption process and the support they need. The focus is upon the children's preparation for placement, moving and settling into the adoptive home, and coping with changes of school, the court process and the maintenance of links with birth relatives and their pasts.

The sample of 41 older adopted children presented an essentially optimistic picture of their adoptive placements. Although some expressed anxieties about their pasts, concerns about their contact arrangements and uneasy feelings of being different from their peers because of their adoptions, overall they spoke positively about having been adopted and about the support they had received from their adoptive parents. However, the study's findings come from older adopted children whose placements were continuing. It did not include the perspectives of those whose placements had disrupted, or whose parents declined to take part because the placements were in difficulty.

The sample

The 41 children who took part in the study were recruited through their adoptive parents who had all participated in the parallel (Lowe and Murch) *Supporting Adoption* study. There were 25 girls and 16 boys. The bias in favour of girls was due to parents passing more invitations to participate in the project to girls rather than to boys. Most of the children were white and placed with white families. Four children were of mixed heritage – one was in a same-race placement and the other three were placed trans-racially. Some of the children had special needs. The parents indicated that eight had learning difficulties, that the same number had behavioural difficulties and that nine had emotional special needs. Two of the children had physical disabilities.

Adoption was the original purpose of the placement for 32 of the 41 children. Six had been placed with long-term foster carers who subsequently applied for adoption and there were three children whose short-term foster placements evolved into long-term arrangements and then into adoption.

Twenty of the children were placed singly although 10 of them had siblings placed in other adoptive and foster families. The other 21 were placed in sibling groups — nine pairs and one group of three. Twelve children were adopted by families with other adopted children. Only six became part of families which included birth children.

The mean age of placement of the group was five years (ranging from two months to 10 years and four months). Once in placement the children waited on average two years and four months before their adoption orders were made. At the time of the interview the children were aged between eight and 15, but most of them (83%) were between eight and 12. On average they had been in the family for five years and eight months. All 41 children were interviewed after their adoption orders had been made. The average length of time between the making of that order and the interview was two years and ten months.

Findings

Communication with children and involving them in the adoption process   The overarching message of the study is that the adults involved in the adoption process need to be sensitive to children's individual needs, particularly by involving them and keeping them informed in a way which takes account of their age, understanding and sense of time. The support offered needs to be underpinned by good adult-child and child-adult communication; but the responsibility for establishing the effective communication lies with the adults.

Many of the children who were interviewed spoke with striking openness and clarity about their past and present wishes and feelings about their placements. The research team believes that the care which they took over four particular aspects of the project had a positive effect on the children's openness. They introduced themselves and the project by using a project leaflet and complementary audio-tape; they used child-friendly tools during the interview; they gave the children assurances about confidentiality and the safe storage of information; and they made sure that the children could influence important aspects of the interview.

Coping with change   With only a few exceptions, the children felt excluded from the general process of being matched and introduced to their adoptive families. In particular, they did not feel included in the preparation or in how they were presented to the families. Over half had experienced painfully long periods between being introduced to the idea of adoption and being matched. The children's comments about their moves to their adoptive homes conveyed a sense of isolation and loneliness. They described how these moves meant significant, simultaneous changes in almost every aspect of their lives. Despite introductory visits, they spoke of the strangeness of their new relationships and environments, including their schools.

Court   Many children had clear memories of going to court and remembered finding the idea of having to go to be frightening and worrying. Social workers' and adoptive parents' reassurances did not always allay their fears. The reality of the hearing, however, was rarely as frightening as the prospect, and the occasion was valued for the outcome of the proceedings. The children also enjoyed their family celebrations afterwards and on the anniversaries of their 'adoption days'.

Links with the past   About 20% of the children had not done life-story work that resulted in a life-story book. However, the majority who had life-story books found them helpful because, as intended, they assisted them in understanding their pasts and in holding on to the threads of their family and placement histories. They appreciated them being kept in easily accessible places and looked at them repeatedly, although because some were only scrap books it seemed unlikely that they would survive intact for long. A few children said, or demonstrated, that they did not understand or retain all the information contained in their books, or conveyed to them during the life-story work itself.

Almost two-thirds of the children had some form of contact with their birth family. When talking about contact some of the children expressed feelings of sadness, loss and loneliness, and unveiled their need for knowledge about their birth families and their pasts. Overall, the children had very clear views about the post-adoption order contact they did or did not have with their birth family members and other people from their pasts. Of those who had contact with their birth relatives, some were content with the current arrangements and some accepted not having contact. Others mentioned that when they were older they hoped to re-establish contact, or have more of it. Some children, however, wanted immediate changes to aspects of their contact. They usually wanted to see more of their birth family members, particularly their mothers and siblings. Some children were mystified by a lack of, or limited, contact with their birth family members or other important people from their pasts, notably foster parents.

Stigmatisation and bullying   Almost a third of the children described being bullied at school. For this and other reasons many were anxious about other children knowing that they were adopted and therefore in some way *different*. However, they did not always feel that they had much control over the spread of information.

Messages for policy and practice

The study's key messages for adults supporting children through the adoption process include the need for them to:

- express themselves simply and clearly when communicating with children about adoption and to match their explanations of new ideas to the children's ages and levels of understanding;
- be aware of the possible impact of emotional distress on children's understanding;
- offer reassurances and encouragement to children about their moves to their adoptive homes;
- try to match the pace of change to the child's pace of change;
- prepare children carefully for court;
- use robust materials for making life-story books;
- plan for the revision and up-dating of life-story work;
- take into account children's powerful and changing wishes and feelings about contact when making contact arrangements;
- keep contact arrangements under review; and
- be sensitive to children's feelings about others knowing that they are adopted.

APPENDIX 2

Publications so far arising from the studies

Becket C, Groothues C, O'Connor T and the ERA team (1998), Adopting from Romania: the Role of Siblings in Adjustment, *Adoption and Fostering*, 22:2: 25–34.

Dance C and Rushton A (1999), Sibling Separation and Contact in Permanent Placement, in Mullender A (ed), *We are Family: Sibling Relationships in Placement and Beyond*, BAAF.

Groothues C, Becket C, O'Connor T and the ERA team (1998), The Outcome of Adoptions from Romania: Predictors of Parental Satisfaction, *Adoption and Fostering*, 22:4: 30–40.

Lowe N, Murch M, Borkowski M, Weaver A, Beckford V and Thomas C (1999), *Supporting Adoption: Reframing the Approach*, BAAF.

Lowe N with Borkowski M, Copner R, Griew K and Murch M (1993), *Freeing for Adoption Provisions*, HMSO (part of the *Pathways to Adoption* project).

Murch M, Lowe N, Borkowski M, Copner R and Griew K (1993), *Pathways to Adoption: Research Project*, HMSO.

O'Connor T, Bredenkamp D, Rutter M and the ERA team (1999), Attachment Disturbances and Disorders in Children Exposed to Early Severe Deprivation, *Infant Ment. Health J*, 20: 10–29.

Owen M (1994), Single-person Adoption: For and Against, *Children and Society*, 8: 151–63.

Owen M (1999), *Novices, Old Hands and Professionals: Adoption by Single People*, BAAF.

Quinton D, Rushton A, Dance C and Mayes D (1998), *Joining New Families: a Study of Adoption and Fostering in Middle Childhood*, Wiley.

Rutter M and the ERA team (1998), Developmental Catch-up and Deficit Following Adoption after Severe Global Early Privation, *J Child Psychol Psychiat*, 39: 465–76.

Rutter M, Anderson-Wood L, Becket C, Bredenkamp D, Castle J, Groothues C, Keaveney L, Lord C, O'Connor T and the ERA team (1999), Quasi-autistic Patterns Following Severe Global Privation, *J Child Psychol Psychiat*, 40: 537–49.

Thomas C, Beckford V with Murch M and Lowe N (1999), *Adopted Children Speaking*, BAAF.

Select bibliography

Listed below are some of the key publications in the adoption field, excluding those arising from the research considered in this report which appear in Appendix 2.

Barn R (1999), White Mothers, Mixed Parentage Children and Child Welfare, *Br J Soc Work*, 29: 269–84.

Barn R (ed) (1999), *Working with Black Children and Adolescents in Need*, BAAF.

Barth R and Berry M (1988), *Adoption and Disruption: Rates, Risks and Responses*, Aldine de Gruyter, NY.

British Agencies for Adoption and Fostering (BAAF) (1997), *Focus on Adoption: a Snapshot of Adoption Patterns in England – 1995*.

BAAF (1998), *Children Adopted from Care: an Examination of Agency Adoptions in England – 1996.*

Brodzinsky D and Schechter M (eds) (1990), *The Psychology of Adoption*, OUP.

Dept of Health (1991), Children Act Regulations and Guidance, vol 9, *Family Placements*, HMSO.

Dept of Health (1995), *Child Protection: Messages from Research*, HMSO.

Dept of Health (1996), *For Children's Sake: an SSI Inspection of Local Authority Adoption Services*, parts 1 and 2.

Dept of Health (1998), *Adoption – Achieving the Right Balance*, cir LAC (98) 20.

Dept of Health and Welsh Office (1992), *Review of Adoption Law: Report to the Ministers of an Independent Working Group*.

Dept of Health et al (1993), *Adoption: the Future*, Cm 2288, HMSO.

Festinger J (1986), *Necessary Risk: a Study of Adoptions and Disrupted Adoptive Placements*, Child Welfare League of America.

Fratter J (1996), *Adoption with Contact: Implications for Policy and Practice*, BAAF.

Fratter J *et al* (1991), *Permanent Family Placement: a Decade of Experience*, BAAF.

Gibbons J *et al* (1995), *Development after Physical Abuse in Early Childhood*, HMSO.

Hill M *et al* (1989), *Achieving Adoption with Love and Money*, Nat Children's Bureau.

Hill M and Shaw M (eds) (1998), *Signposts in Adoption: Policy, Practice and Research Issues*, BAAF.

Howe D (1998), *Patterns of Adoption*, Blackwell.

Kirk H (1964), *Shared Fate: a Theory of Adoption and Mental Health*, Free Press, NY.

Lambert L *et al* (1990), *Freeing Children for Adoption*, BAAF.

Maugham B *et al* (1998), School Achievement and Adult Qualifications among Adoptees: a Longitudinal Study, *J Child Psychol Psychiat*, 39: 669–85.

McRoy R (1994), *Changing Practice in Adoption*, Hogg Found. Ment. Health, Texas.

Mullender A (ed) (1991), *Open Adoption: the Philosophy and Practice*, BAAF.

Mullender A (ed) (1999), *We are Family: Sibling Relations in Placement and Beyond*, BAAF.

Phillips R and McWilliam E (1996), *After Adoption: Working with Adoptive Families*, BAAF.

Quinton D *et al* (1997), Contact between Children Placed Away from Home and their Birth Parents: Research Issues and Evidence, *Clinical Child Psychol Psychiat*, 2: 393–413.

Quinton D and Selwyn J (1998), Contact with Birth Families in Adoption: a Response to Ryburn, *Child and Family Law Quart*, 10: 349–61.

Ryburn M (1994), *Open Adoption: Research, Theory and Practice*, Avebury.

Ryburn M (1998), In Whose Best Interest? Post-Adoption Contact with the Birth Family, *Child and Family Law Quart*, 10: 53–70.

Sellick C and Thoburn J (1997), *What Works in Family Placement?* Barnardos.

Thoburn J (1994), *Child Placement: Principles and Practice*, Avebury.

Thoburn J et al (1986), *Permanence in Child Care*, OUP.

Triseliotis J and Russell J (1984), *Hard to Place: the Outcome of Adoption and Residential Care*, Gower.

Triseliotis J et al (1997), *Adoption: Theory, Policy and Practice*, Cassell.

Various relevant articles appear in the following journals:

Adoption and Fostering
British Journal of Social Work
Child and Family Law Quarterly
Child and Family Social Work
Child Welfare (US)
Children and Society
Journal of Child Psychology and Psychiatry

Related titles of interest...

WILEY

Working in Children's Homes
Challenges and Complexities
DOROTHY WHITAKER, LESLEY ARCHER and LESLIE HICKS, all of University of York, UK

This book looks at the reality of working in a children's home and what the staff face on a day-to-day basis. The range of tasks and how these tasks accumulate during the day is examined alongside the rewards and stresses of residential work. It deals with children and young people in residential care - their personal characteristics, life stage and behaviour on entering. Working with individual young people, working with a mix of young people and working with and being managed by a large organisation is covered - including legal and jurisdiction issues. The book closes with a look at the quality of practice, of outcomes for young people and homes, and implications for the future.

0471 979538   262pp   April 1998   Paperback

Joining New Families
A Study of Adoption and Fostering in Middle Childhood
DAVID QUINTON, University of Bristol, ALAN RUSHTON, Maudsley Hospital, London, UK, CHERILYN DANCE and DEBORAH MAYES, both of Maudsley Family Research Studies, Institute of Psychiatry, London

This book investigates the two most prominent forms of action taken when children have suffered abuse or neglect by their parents. First the idea that alternative permanent family placements, through adoption, with complete severance of all ties with the natural parents is discussed, and second, the more . open view of adoption where the child's origins are acknowledged and discussed, and contact between the child and birth parents is maintained and investigated. This book is based on the findings of the comprehensive and prestigious Maudsley Adoption and Fostering Study commissioned by the Department of Health. It summarises the results of this survey and makes suggestions for future placements and policy.

0471 97837 X   282pp   November 1998   Paperback